MIRACLE & ITS
PHILOSOPHICAL
PRESUPPOSITIONS

MIRACLE & ITS PHILOSOPHICAL PRESUPPOSITIONS

THREE LECTURES DELIVERED
IN THE UNIVERSITY OF LONDON
1924

by

F. R. TENNANT, D.D., B.Sc.

FELLOW AND LECTURER OF
TRINITY COLLEGE, CAMBRIDGE

Author of
The Concept of Sin
etc.

CAMBRIDGE
AT THE UNIVERSITY PRESS
1925

CAMBRIDGE
UNIVERSITY PRESS

University Printing House, Cambridge CB2 8BS, United Kingdom

Cambridge University Press is part of the University of Cambridge.

It furthers the University's mission by disseminating knowledge in the pursuit of education, learning and research at the highest international levels of excellence.

www.cambridge.org
Information on this title: www.cambridge.org/9781316633397

First published 1925
First paperback edition 2016

A catalogue record for this publication is available from the British Library

ISBN 978-1-316-63339-7 Paperback

CONTENTS

Lecture I

MIRACLE AND THE REIGN
OF LAW

THE subject which I have chosen for this short course of Lectures does not belong to the class of burning questions: neither the possibility nor the actuality of the miraculous is at present a topic around which controversy is directly engaged, though as a side-issue involved in other living problems it may be regarded as a smouldering fire. It is connected, however, with several presuppositions that are of perennial interest to students of what is called 'philosophy of religion' and might more aptly be designated 'philosophical theology.' It raises ulterior questions such as the meaning of the phrase 'reign of law,' the nature of inductive science and its relation to religious belief, the compatibility of providential guidance of the physical world with a relatively settled natural order, the identity and the difference between theism and deism: and indeed a number of closely connected issues comprised in the many-sided problem of the relation of God to the world and man. It is partly because the subject of miracle furnishes a text for a discourse on such matters that I have adopted it. But that is not the sole reason. The long controversy concerning miracle will always possess historical interest; and inasmuch as some two hundred years of discussion by philosophers, men of science and theologians left the subject in a state of confusion, it is desirable that some straightening out be undertaken. I propose, therefore, to try to disentangle some issues that were intertwined, and to discuss them separately.

The different aspects of miracle which successively received emphasis, as external pressure obliged Christian apologetic to take on new forms, are already discernible in the primitive or pre-scientific notion of the miraculous. That notion was constructed by popular thought, and for practical and religious rather than for theoretical and scientific purposes. It is not to be expected, therefore, to be a definite and precise concept. As we shall presently see, it is when we try to make it one that our difficulties begin. The original signification of 'miracle' is a wonder; and we still use the word in this primitive sense when, in common parlance, we speak of a great work of art as a miracle. In the idea of the wonderful, we may observe, there inheres from the first a two-fold reference—the source of an ambiguity which we shall later be concerned to eliminate—viz. a relation to other objects and a relation to human subjects. Wonderfulness resolves itself into unprecedentedness or novelty, and sometimes connotes rarity, which are objective traits; but also into impressiveness, which is a matter of subjective attitude towards an object, and a quality which an object cannot possess unless someone is impressed by it. In the former of these elements into which wonderfulness may be resolved, we detect implicit reference to a background of the ordinary against which the wonder appears as extraordinary, and therefore the germ of the later explicit contrast between miracle and a settled order. The latter mark of impressiveness almost exclusively constitutes the wonder as it was generally conceived by the ancient Hebrew mind. When, in the Old Testament, attention is called to 'the wonders He hath done,' there seems often to be no hint of even implicit antithesis between the wonder and the order of Nature, no suggestion of unprecedentedness or rarity. The wonders of the Old Testament might be said to be practically equivalent to the 'signs' of New Testament writers if we had right to believe that for those writers any event would have been a sign had it not been also somewhat of a wonder.

The remaining mark of the miracle, as it came to be conceived in theology, viz. divine authorship, we should not expect to find in the notion in so far as it was shaped before monotheism emerged, or theological apologetic was called for.

In the pre-scientific age, before the conception of a reign of law or Nature's uniformity pervaded common thought, there could be no difficulty about giving credence to the marvellous; and no hard line could be drawn between the natural and the supernatural. But when uniformity came not only to be explicitly recognised but also to be scientifically formulated, the mark of novelty or extraordinariness required to be made more precise. The marvellous, in order to possess evidential value as to divine interposition, needed, in a scientific age, to be conceived as the unaccountable, as evincing inexplicability in terms of natural law. Events such as the devastating earthquake, at once rare and impressive, became attributable to Nature's unaided potencies, and no longer required postulation of intrusive divine agency. If an alleged miracle, therefore, was to be regarded as proving such direct agency, while an earthquake did not, it needed to be conceived not only as marvellous but also as unique in respect of its causation, and consequently as standing in contrast with the ordinary or settled course of Nature, the nexus of secondary causes. Thus clarification and definition such as was started when theology became confronted with the scientific insistence on law and regularity, inevitably led to the whole issue becoming vastly complicated through inclusion of reference to causation.

We shall find that when, in more recent times, difficulties increasingly beset the characterisation of miracle on its objective side, or in respect of its abnormality and its non-natural causation, the subjective aspect of impressiveness, and the function of causing faith rather than that of proving knowledge, came again to receive emphasis. But meanwhile we may consider how the difficulties to which I have alluded emerged, as theology sought to render definite and intellectually serviceable the vague notion of miracle which it had inherited from pre-scientific belief.

It will conduce to clearness of exposition to pursue historical or chronological order as far as possible, but to deviate from it and take up the logical instead, when pursuit of the latter order becomes essential for the better understanding of any stage in the controversy concerning miracle. And it will not be necessary to go further back in time than the era at which modernity may be

said to have begun in English theology, viz.
the rise of eighteenth-century deism*, save
to indicate in few words the position, with
regard to miracle, of the orthodoxy which
the deists unsettled.

At that time, viz. about 1700, a certain kind
of rational or natural theology was generally
believed to be absolutely beyond question.
Locke, with some reservations, had upheld
it; the deists could cite pillars of orthodoxy
as professing it and themselves accepted it
as self-evident or at least characterised by
rigorous demonstrability; and Butler treated
proof of its tenets as superfluous. The scrip-
tures were with practical unanimity regarded
as sacrosanct, and their statements as admitting of no kind of doubt. The whole system
of dogmatic theology was accepted by the
intellectual, whether men of letters or of
science, philosophers or statesmen. Accordingly, there was no question, from within
the Church, as to the actual occurrence of
at least the gospel miracles, and in them was
seen an overwhelming proof of the Christian
revelation. Suspicion that all was not well
with this received theology, save the part
called natural, was first expressed by Toland,
Tindal, and other of those free-lances who
received the name of deists; and in course
of time that suspicion concentrated on

* See Note A, p. 96.

miracles. The earliest of this group of writers did not expressly repudiate the miraculous: but it was soon realised that their presuppositions involved its super-fluousness, and indeed implied its impossibility. Eighteenth-century deism, we may note by the way, is not to be confounded with the particular theory as to God's relation to the world which received the name of deism in philosophy. Toland and Tindal, I presume, were not read by writers of the subsequent century; if so, that would explain the fact that the deists in the historical sense of the term came to be regarded as professed deists in the philosophical sense. That is a mistake; for the theory in question was expressly repudiated, and even called atheism, by them as well as by their seventeenth-century predecessors. That it was implied in their natural theology, they did not realise. Thus the deist of the early eighteenth century would be better described as a rational theist. Another mistake still current as to these writers, is that they were disciples of Locke. In so far as Locke was an empiricist, they were not of his school, though there was much in common between his theology and theirs. Indeed, such philosophical presuppositions as the deists vaguely disclose were rather those of rationalism, of the kind taught by Spinoza or the Leibniz-Wolffians.

This is particularly evident in their conception of laws of Nature; and inasmuch as that conception involves a notion of law which played an important part during the earlier stage of the miracle-controversy, it will be well to bring it under scrutiny. Thus we may make a beginning, historically and logically, of investigation of what has been meant, and what should be meant by 'the reign of law.'

As rationalists, the early deists believed that there existed a body of truth about the actual world that had been discovered by reason, or the *lumen naturale* alone, and was characterised by the same kind of necessity as pertains to mathematical theorems, or to the relations between propositions dealt with in the pure sciences. Natural law was among the contents of this supposed knowledge; and for the deists as for their rationalistic predecessors, 'law' connoted necessity. They speak of law, physical and ethical, as part of the constitution imposed once and for all upon the world by God; and sometimes as an eternal *prius*, existing before the world was, and which it was 'fitting' for God to recognise. As it is only on this presupposition as to the meaning of 'law' that miracle and, speaking more generally, divine providence or immanence, can be ruled out as impossible, it behoves us to examine the logical value and the epistemological basis of the notion.

We understand what is meant by necessity, as applied to propositions, though we cannot define it because it is ultimate and irreducible to simpler ideas. The only criterion by which necessity can be recognised when present, is self-evidence to developed reason; and in the case of derived or inferred propositions, the relation of logical implication to truth that is self-evident. In pure geometry, for instance, such necessary truth is verily encountered; there we can lay foundations by positing definitions, and we can establish connexions between them possessing all the necessity of logical implication. It is quite another question, however, whether we meet with any such truth in the applied or the empirical sciences concerned with actuality. For there we do not begin by laying foundations: the foundations are laid for us already, being posited in the willy-nilly data of sense-impression, the primary reality from which physical science sets out in its construction of knowledge of the external world. There we do not start from definitions and pure concepts, but from obscure concepts fashioned for practical purposes by common sense.

Science and philosophy can only begin *in mediis rebus*. The extremest of rationalists really began so, though in the exposition of their systems they set out from the finished product of their thought, the pure concept. Rationalism had attained its climax in Spinoza who naïvely assumed the order and connexion of pure ideas to be identical with the order and connexion of things, and *causa* to be identical with *ratio*. Hence it was natural for representatives of the rationalistic school to assert that laws concerning actuality were characterised by logical necessity*. And this was the more natural because

---

* As an instance of logical necessity, we may take that of the proposition 'if all swans are white, no black bird is a swan.' This would be necessarily true if there were black swans, or no swans; it asserts no fact, and presupposes no empirical observation. Similarly, the laws of kinematics, etc., may assert necessary relations between concepts such as space, time and motion; they assert nothing as to the concrete filling of space and time, or as to actuality. Laws of Nature, on the other hand, do make statements as to actuality, and before any such statements can be made, actuality must be consulted. Science, as distinguished from logic or pure mathematics, can only be wise after the event. If it define matter as what occupies space, there is no *a priori* certainty that matter has inertia, as there is that in a triangle the angles are equal to two right angles. Whether stationary matter can be made to move, or moving matter be made to stop moving, can in the first instance be ascertainable only by experiment; matter, not our thought, decides such questions. Occupation of space does not imply movability; and the proposition that 'if a billiard-ball be struck, it will move,' is not characterised by *a priori* necessity independent of observation, like the proposition about

mathematics was still regarded as the ideal, *i.e.* the paradigm, of science, instead of as an ideal science in the sense of knowledge about ideas. Ideas in a pure science may be never so clear and distinct, and propositions about them never so logically knit together into a self-consistent system; yet it is quite another question whether the system will have any validity of actuality or brute fact. So far from there being identity between the orders of idea and fact, there is no *a priori*

swans. For all we *know*, we may at any moment come across a billiard-ball that no one can move; though the *probability* is that we shall not. If it be the case that billiard-balls are necessarily movable, this is not because we are pleased to think so, but because of the actual nature of balls, which conceivably might have been different from what experience has found it to be. Thus nomic necessity is only bestowed on a proposition by the determinate nature of the actualities to which the proposition refers; it has nothing to do with concepts or with logic, and that it has been confounded with the necessity of logical implication seems to be due to the surreptitious invoking of brute fact without which necessary truth never acquires purchase on actuality. Further, the necessity ascribed to a law of Nature is always conditional on our assumptions as to the ultimate constitution of Nature being true when they are not demonstrable. No law of Nature asserts categorically that anything must happen; only that it will happen if certain conditions continue: and that these conditions will continue is in the last resort matter of mere expectation. Common sense is apt to confound its practical and psychological certitude as to the sun's rising to-morrow with logical certainty or necessary truth; but logically there is no connexion.

reason why there should even be any correspondence. There may be, and there may
not be. Whether there is, and to what extent
there is, can only be found out by comparing
the two, by experiment. This must be so, I
repeat, because actuality is not posited by
us, like the geometer's lines without breadth;
it is posited for us and thrust upon us willy-
nilly, and so cannot wholly be fashioned
a priori. Hume's insistence on this truth
may be regarded as one of the most momentous crises in the whole history of philosophy.
Kant professed to have been aroused from
dogmatic slumber by Hume's trumpet-blast;
but, like Dr Watts' sluggard, he was wakened
too soon and must slumber again. In other
words, Kant's rationalistic prejudices were
insuperable, and led him to waste his energies
on an attempt to elaborate the conditions
of a pure science of Nature. Less shrewd
than Newton himself, he believed that pure
or necessary knowledge of Nature lay to
hand in Newtonian physics. He was enabled
to cherish that illusion only because he had
surreptitiously smuggled into his storehouse
of pure ideas concepts such as inertia, de-
rivable only from sense-experience, which
have no place there. We are now able to see
clearly that Kant failed to intrench within
science the rationalism that he had expelled
from theology; we have learned, since his

day, too much about the nature of scientific induction to be able to retain the Kantian confidence*. But more of that anon.

Returning to the rationalistic presuppositions of the deists, we can now assert that their assumption of a reign of law in the sense of an all-pervading, unconditional, immutable necessity binding all things fast in fate, is groundless. Their belief that such a system of law existed prior to actuality and even to God, involves the further fallacy of confounding the valid with the separately existent, and the *universale in re* with the *universale ante rem*. There can be no preexistent mould of law into which being has to fit, or be fitted by God, in order to be; in the case of the existent and what is valid of the existent, there is no 'before or after other,' temporally or logically. Facts do not presuppose laws, but laws facts. Or, more correctly, there is no presupposing either way, but co-supposing. As Boutroux happily expresses it, if laws are the channels along which the stream of fact rushes, the channels have themselves been hollowed by the facts.

We may assert, then, that the possibility of miracle as an exception to law is not precluded *a priori*. Of law that could so preclude miracle, we know nothing: unless

* See Note B, p. 98.

indeed it should prove that empirical and inductive methods can yield knowledge of actuality possessing the unconditional certainty that would have characterised the rationalist's pure science of Nature had he succeeded in establishing it. Whether this is so or not, shall presently be discussed in the light of quite recent and decisive knowledge as to the fundamental issues involved. But that discussion can best be approached by considering the classical attempt of the nineteenth century to inflate empirical science into an equivalent to the obsolete *a priori* systems of the two preceding centuries.

This brings us to what we may distinguish as the second phase of the controversy concerning miracle, if we confine ourselves as yet to its philosophical aspect. During the first stage of the controversy the prepossessions in virtue of which the possibility of miracle had been denied were rationalistic; during the second, they were what may be called pseudo-scientific, though to describe them so is to anticipate the conclusion which I hope to establish. Throughout the period with which we are now to be concerned, confidence in the prestige and the all-sufficiency of scientific method outstripped critical knowledge as to the logical structure of science, and valour lacked its better part.

We may note in passing that Hume, who,

as we shall see later, did not scruple in his essay on miracles to assume the uniformity of Nature as if it were an *a priori* principle, was too shrewd to try to prove its universality. His less cautious disciple, J. S. Mill, was, however, as audacious in zeal to prove as the master had been, upon occasion, to assume.

In Mill's time the method of inductive science, in its logical aspect, was generally conceived to be a syllogistic process involving the principle of uniformity as its major premiss. Investigators in the field of science such as made pronouncements on method may be said to have been unanimous as to that principle underlying all scientific procedure; and Mill exerted a wide and powerful influence, not only upon men of science but also on theologians and the general public, when he argued that the uniformity principle, itself presupposed in all problematical induction, could be proved cumulatively by particular inductions. It is not necessary to repeat Mill's argumentation; readers of his *Logic* will be familiar with his constant begging of the question by appropriating unconditional or universal terms such as 'invariable,' for the description of Nature's behaviour, while all that his empiricism warranted was the very different phrase 'hitherto unvarying.' The universal, which by no manner of means could be extracted out of the particular, was thus illicitly foisted into it; just as the rationalist of an earlier day had always clandestinely invoked the sensory in order to get under weigh with his pure concepts. Mill's failure is now as evident as that of Kant who sought the same goal from the opposite direction. But his generation, somewhat obsessed by the rapid progress of the physical sciences, was easily persuaded that inductive science had succeeded where rationalistic philosophy had failed; and that it had established a reign of law as rigorous and as knowable as that the deist had conceived. Carlyle was typical of his time in asserting it to be 'as sure as mathematics' that such a thing as a miracle had never happened. In the theological world this doctrine was advocated by Baden-Powell, author of an article in *Essays and Reviews* which dealt with miracle; and the controversy on miracle was conducted for years between opponents equally pledged to this pseudo-scientific belief, which indeed is not yet everywhere put away. Baden-Powell magnified the inductive principle into the equivalent of an *a priori* axiom, and so granted to science a capacity to disparage alleged miracle which science had no right to claim. What some theologians thus conceded was repudiated in the name of science by the agnostic Huxley. But there arose also from the camp of conservative Christian theology a doughty vindicator of miracle against this pseudo-scientific attack. In his Bampton Lectures on Miracle, Prof. Mozley put forth by far the ablest defence of miracle, as the orthodoxy of his day conceived it, that was forthcoming in the nineteenth century. He nailed his colours, it is true, to a mast which has since disappeared beneath the waves of critical research. But from such a standpoint as could then reasonably be adopted, Mozley wrote with a vigour and a masterly clearness that stand favourably contrasted with the vagueness and vacillation of contemporary apologists. He was especially concerned to refute the position represented by Baden-Powell and supported by the logic of Mill; and he appealed from Mill the disciple to Hume the master. The uniformity of Nature, he argued, the dogma that natural law tells us what always has been, will be, and must be, is not a rational, *i.e.* a self-evident or demonstrable truth, though it may be an irresistible belief for many minds. Reid had no right to call it the outcome of 'instinctive prescience,' for it issues rather from instinctive expectation. In order to know it to be a rational principle, we should need to be completely conversant with the ultimate structure of the world. Rationalists and deists had tacitly claimed to possess such knowledge, but modern science knew better. If induction be not the same as deduction from proved premisses, but is a calculus of probability, we cannot exclude the unlikely or the supra-normal as impossible or unworthy of all credence. If the principle of uniformity be not rational, belief in miracle is not irrational.

It is instructive that a critic of the order of the late Prof. Bruce perpetuated Baden-Powell's error after Mozley had so clearly exposed it. Quoting with approval the author of *Supernatural Religion,* Bruce asserts that 'an order is both necessary and fatal to miracle.' This is to confound the invariable regularity of *a priorism* with the problematic regularity of which science has knowledge; and the confusion seems to be ineradicable to-day from many minds whose acquaintance with science and its logic is superficial.

Mozley's argument, in so far as I have reproduced it, is unanswerable. Its cogency has indeed become more evident since the foundations of induction, obscure enough in Mill's generation, have been clearly illumined. Allusion to this recent research, which has important bearing on matter more significant to philosophical theology than the subject of miracle, has already been promised; and

logical order requires discussion of it at this
point.

Already in the last century logicians were
finding the vague principle of uniformity
incapable of being stated in a form that is
plausible and practically serviceable rather
than merely platitudinous or tautological.
They had also established that whatever this
obscure principle exactly meant, it was no
more than a postulate. This conclusion was
afterwards supported by the psychologist,
who stepped in to testify to the humble origin
of the principle in man's primordial credulity.
It was first hoped for, in piecemeal measure,
and gradually became experientially sub-
stantiated. It was the outcome of human
adventurousness, of the habit of mind expressed in *credo ut intelligam*, or 'nothing
venture, nothing have.' But the present
century has witnessed a further development. The Cambridge logicians, Mr Johnson,
Mr Keynes and Dr Broad, have succeeded
in replacing the uniformity-postulate by an
inductive principle and one or two specific
propositions concerning the ultimate constitution of the physical world. In the old
postulate, we now see, there lay concealed,
conjoined and confused, several assumptions
which are mutually independent and are
respectively patient of clear and distinct
formulation. Briefly summarised, one of

these is that Nature is built up of few natural kinds or substances, all the instances of any one of which are *exactly* alike and *completely* permanent. Note here the unconditional universals which, as we have already seen, necessarily transcend empirical observation. The other is that each elementary change, constituent of a molar physical change, is independently caused, so that to physical causation there applies a principle similar to the parallelogram law in the case of forces and velocities. It is obvious that neither of these propositions is self-evident or capable of proof, inductively or deductively. They are called probable. But it should be observed, as a matter of far-reaching import, that the word 'probable' is then used in a sense quite different from that which it bears when denoting the logical relation of probability subsisting, for instance, between the fundamental theories of physics and these inductive presuppositions themselves. What alone can be meant in calling these latter principles probable is that they are *suggested* by Nature's behaviour and that the more thoroughly Nature is explored, and the more precisely natural laws are formulated, the more exact is the correspondence between the laws and the facts. This probability, which we now see to be the guide of science as well as the guide of life, is thus a non-logical affair. Psychologically, it is sanguine hope or expectation, certitude or subjective convincedness, not logical or objective certainty. Metaphysically, it is assumption as to the unseen and the unverifiable. Science, as well as religious faith, is at bottom the substantiation of things hoped for, the pragmatic evidencing of things not seen. Thus in our own day the logician has removed for ever from the reach of either the philosopher or the devotee of science rightly or wrongly so-called, the instrument by which was fashioned, sometimes by the one, sometimes by the other, the reign of law in the one sense of 'law' that we have as yet been studying—viz. that of immutable connexion characterising all change in a closed system.

We may turn now to the other chief meaning of this term 'law'—the one which it bears when used in the inductive science of to-day. Scientific thought had, as a matter of fact, rejected and disowned the *a priori* instrument before the logician recently relegated it to the museum of obsolete armoury. Physicists themselves have for some time been insisting that natural law, as invoked by science, is quite different from the rationalist's law connoting universal necessity. At this point we may revert to historical order of exposition and, tracing the influence of scientific thought on the shaping of the theological idea of miracle, consider what became some decades ago the current meaning of 'law' as used in the physical sciences.

Laws of Nature, we are told by physicists of repute, are not *a priori* prescriptions, but empirically devised descriptions—of similarities, etc. As to their verbal form they undergo remodelling as knowledge increases. They briefly or economically subsume Nature's more or less recent behaviour in so far as it has been observed up to date and no further. Laws, as known up to a certain hour, may perfectly well be broken; and a broken law is but an inadequate description. If an exception to a law turns up, whether it be the behaviour of radium or the resuscitation of the dead to life, we must, if we can, widen the law to include the abnormal case.

As this conception of law and its relatively limited scope passed from scientific into theological literature as a substitute for the meaning with which 'law' had previously been used, the character of the controversy about miracle underwent a change. Law still continued, indeed, to obsess thought and to receive the adulatory reverence to which it was entitled only in case it bespoke universal necessity; hence the anxiety of popular theology to credit both miracles and their divine Agent with law-abidingness by resorting to 'higher laws' which were supposed to be obeyed when natural laws were 'violated': a conception which we shall examine presently. But theologians were now enabled to see that science itself had put an end to the dogma of the impossibility of miracle. This gain, as we shall find, was attended with theological loss; which loss in turn sometimes escaped discernment, so that controversy became further confused. The loss to which I refer is that of a criterion by which any given marvel may be recognised as a miracle in such a sense as to warrant for it evidential value for proving supernatural intervention.

This, however, is to anticipate the results of inquiry into another department of our subject than that which is now before us. Confining myself for the present to the scientific idea of law, I will bring the discussion of it up to date.

The word 'description,' which I have used once or twice, is taken so seriously in some quarters, is so charged with intentional antithesis to 'explanation' of the causal kind, that we might fairly bestow the title of 'descriptionist school' upon an influential group of recent writers on natural philosophy. We are only concerned now with the application of the term 'description' to laws of

Nature; not with its bearing on the real or ideal status of scientific concepts such as those of potential energy or electron. In the former connexion, I would venture to advise theologians not to be too hasty to accept what may look like a boon from their scientific friends. Of course the sense in which 'description' has been used by men of science is technical. It would only be cavilling about a word to point out that scientific laws or conceptual descriptions, in that they are selective and inexhaustive, emphasising one aspect of phenomena and ignoring others because negligible for a specific purpose, are not descriptive in the ordinary sense of that term. But it is important to observe that unless a natural law be more than a description, even in the new specialised and technical sense, it is impossible for science to justify its own method with all its practical success. For that method and its results certainly presuppose a relatively stable nexus in phenomena, which the word 'description' simply ignores. Science, I would contend, is more penetrative than the language of some of its own representatives serves to suggest. It has repeatedly been stated by leaders of the descriptionist school that description consists solely in saying 'how' things happen, and that 'how' means no more than 'like what.' It means that; but, as it seems to me, it means more also: viz. by issuing out of so and so, and by issuing, after an interval of time, in so and so. The descriptionist has eliminated the term 'cause,' like the term 'explanation,' from his vocabulary, as denoting a metaphysical fetish; but inasmuch as science is knowledge of a stable nexus of relations between perceptual data—relations which, as well as the particular data themselves, enter into the structure of the physical—the anathematised concept of cause or actual connexion is presupposed all the time in his thought and his experimenting. Otherwise laws would have no validity, nor science any predictiveness. A 'relatively settled order' is the element of fact with which natural theology is confronted; and I fail to see how the philosophy of science, any more than theology, can afford to ignore it. Descriptionism, as represented by Mach and Karl Pearson, Ward, Poynting and Hobson, is perhaps merely a methodological profession that science has no concern with the nature of the activity-nexus in the world, and can ignore it for its own departmental purpose. In that case descriptionism is harmless—so long as it does not imply that what it agrees to leave aside is not there. But it is no instrument for the natural theologian's use. For while the theologian may be grateful to science for its confession that of laws that never shall be broken, or even of laws that shall persist till to-morrow, it knows nothing, having no more than sanguine expectation with regard to them, he has to reckon with the fact that at any rate within certain tracts of the universe and for a certain time-interval, laws and regularity have been actually found to obtain; and with the further fact that such empirical regularity must have a sufficient reason.

In the light of the foregoing account of the gradual clarification of the nature of natural law, we can clearly see that statements concerning law wait upon statements concerning fact, and not *vice versa*. We can now perhaps clearly understand why, during the last century, controversy shifted from the question as to the possibility of miracle to that of its actuality. The move was dictated by science. In the first stage of the dispute, the miraculous was attacked on the ground of its *a priori* impossibility. When the rationalistic meaning of law became obsolete, the nature of scientific induction was still so imperfectly ascertained by the wise and so gravely misunderstood by the unwise, that miracle continued for a time to be branded as impossible because violating law. At length, after self-examination, science came to refuse, and to refuse sometimes with vehement indignation, to allow its prestige to be claimed for *a priorism* of the pseudo-scientific type. From that day the verdict 'miracles cannot happen' began to be replaced by 'miracles do not happen.' And if scientific method, applied thenceforward increasingly in literary and historical research, favoured the insinuation lurking in Matthew Arnold's dictum, that miracles never did happen, it did so on other grounds with which we are not just yet to be concerned.

Before we leave the subject of law and its bearing on miracle, the notion of 'higher laws,' already alluded to, demands brief consideration. For though the conception is obsolete, discussion of it will be found to open out another issue which has as yet only been mentioned to be postponed. The idea of higher laws is one to which apologists of the nineteenth century resorted when they misunderstood science to proclaim events not reducible to law to be unworthy of human credence if not unworthy of divine authorship. While conserving the alleged marvels of scripture, they would throw a sop to science by claiming for such facts obedience to law in spite of disobedience to such law as science knew. Bishop Butler had invoked 'general laws of wisdom' as laws of God's nature; and with like intention one of the

best writers of the nineteenth century on
miracle, Bushnell, used the phrase 'the law
of the end.'* These, for a theist, are legitimate conceptions; but they have nothing
in common with the higher laws of *things*
incompatible with natural law. Mozley
observed that the phrase 'higher laws' might
bear more than one meaning. For instance,
it might be so used as to suggest that the
apparently non-natural event really had
connexion, as yet unknown, with known
law. Such is actually the case, at least tem-
porarily, whenever science stumbles upon a
new kind of fact, such as the Röntgen ray.
But if this were all that reference to higher
law was intended to signify, the outcome
would be that for any alleged miracle a
natural explanation might in time be forthcoming. That would involve surrender of the
evidential value of miracle, the one function
which was then generally deemed essential
to miracle. Popular writers on the virgin-
birth of our Lord sometimes evince a similar
confusion to-day: miraculous birth is asserted
to insure Christ's non-inheritance of original
sin or His actual sinlessness; and it is then
represented that this miracle is not contrary
to Nature in that it is paralleled by normal
parthenogenesis in the lower animals. It is

* Cf. Augustine, *Contra Faust.* xxvi., and Aquinas,
Summa, I. cv. Art. 6.

thus overlooked that in order that a miracle may have any significance for dogmatic theology it must have that incompatibility with natural law which, in the dogmatic interest, has been asserted, and, in the pseudo-scientific interest, has been withdrawn.

More probably, however, 'higher law' was intended to denote something more than law according to which a miracle may be conceived as only seeming to conflict with ordinary law. It seems rather to denote a system of law unknown and unknowable to us, sufficiently comprehensive to include both the settled order and the anomaly. It then appears to involve the notion, which we have seen to be fallacious, of a *prius* of law lying in wait for instances. But whether this be so or not, the arbitrary supposition that there are such higher laws is irrelevant to the problem, so long as the criterion of miracle is taken to be incompatibility with such law as we do know. The resolution of natural abnormalities into higher normalities is beside the issue.

Reference to this device of a bygone day will have served to emphasise the conclusion to which our historical study has so far brought us: viz. that in order to evidence supernatural agency, the miracle must itself be supernatural in the sense of being incapable of subsumption under laws with which science is acquainted. Something more than this is contained in the concept of the supernatural, and consequently in that of miracle, which is to receive full consideration in my next lecture. But so far as our first approximation to a definition of miracle goes, and whatever else a miracle must be, it is a happening not reducible to law.

No sooner, however, have we taken this first step towards a definition of miracle such as shall be theologically significant and scientifically definite, than the need presents itself to refine; and our difficulties begin to be manifest. For the phrase 'reducible to law' is ambiguous. A law of Nature, in the only sense in which we have found it legitimate to use the expression, is provisional and capable of being revised or superseded; it is an account of some part of Nature's behaviour up to date. Events not reducible to law in one generation may become so reducible at a later time. If this is what is to be implied by our phrase, the further definition of miracle must resolve the ambiguity with which we are confronted, by inserting a qualification involving reference to the stage of knowledge attained by a given generation or by certain individuals. If, on the other hand, 'not reducible' is to mean absolutely and for all time irreducible, no such qualification is necessary; but as we shall presently see, the definition of miracle then becomes theologically worthless. Here then we have arrived at a parting of the ways. We must decide between two alternatives. Are we to retain a concept which, taking account of the subjective aspect, becomes of less or (to avoid the controversial) of different theological value, from that of the concept which we had provisionally reached: or are we to adopt one which, for reasons to be adduced later, is of no value at all?

Attending for the present to the former alternative alone, let us note its consequences. Acts of healing mediated through the mind and the faith of the patient are recorded of our Lord, and have passed for miracles evidencing His divine nature; to-day such acts are commonly performed by faith-healers, agnostic as well as Christian. What was a miracle for the first generation of Christians is thus no miracle to us. The same seems to be the case with the stigmata of St Francis of Assisi. The unbeliever in the supernatural no longer need resort to violent treatment of the historical evidence that the stigmata were actually visible on the saint's body; for we are now told that similar wounds can be produced, by certain individuals and in certain circumstances, on the right spots of the body, according to the laws of auto-suggestion. Thus a gap which exists in Nature's regularity as it is known at any particular time, then leaving room for interpretation in terms of miracle, may close up as our knowledge of Nature increases. And theoretically, no limit can be assigned to such reduction to law of the once apparently irreducible. If science already cherishes the hope of being able to synthesise living matter out of the inorganic, it is not absurd for the scientific imagination to entertain the possibility even of resuscitating life in an organised body from which life has but recently departed. The discovery of natural means of producing effects which once passed for miracles does not logically imply that bygone marvels were not wrought by supernatural means; but it removes all ground for logical certainty that they were so produced. We may point to events that are not causally to be connected with the natural order by the science of a given day; but we cannot affirm that any such event is really excluded from the causal nexus that exists but which we only know in part. Science thus leaves theology free to assert the possibility of miracle; but she seems to preclude the possibility of our being able to pronounce a marvel to be a miracle in the objective or absolute sense of the word: the sense, *i.e.*, in which it denotes incapability for all time of being subsumed under natural law. Until we shall have arrived at something like omniscience as to Nature's constitution and intrinsic capacities, we cannot affirm any marvel to be beyond them.

We have now come in sight of new issues: those, namely, of the causation and the knowability of miracle. These are subjects for discussion on future occasions; and I would bring the present lecture to its conclusion by emphasising the fact which we have been led to apprehend, that laws of Nature and miracle both inevitably involve reference to human knowledge in its successively passing stages as well as to the constitution of the world and the assumed fixity thereof. It is of historical interest to note that this fact was recognised by the shrewd common sense of Locke, though it seems to have escaped the subtler intellect of Aquinas. A comparison of statements of these two philosophers will serve to make clearer the point with which we have been concerned.

Aquinas undertakes to expound Augustine's definition of a miracle*: 'When God does anything against that order of Nature which we know and are accustomed to

* *Summa*, I. cv. Art. 7. (Translation by Fathers of the Eng. Dominican Province, Third Number, p. 405.)

observe, we call it a miracle.' He rightly
remarks that a thing is wonderful to one
man and not to another: 'an eclipse is to a
rustic, but not to an astronomer.' But he
immediately proceeds to distinguish the
miracle from the marvel by attributing it
to 'a cause absolutely hidden from all.' He
is obviously not alive to the immense difference between this assertion and the definition
which he has cited and is explaining. Of
causes *absolutely* hidden, or incapable of ever
being discovered within Nature, as we have
seen, we have no right to speak. Locke is
more cautious and consistent. In his essay
on miracle, he expressly objects to the usual
definition, *i.e.* 'an extraordinary operation
performable by God alone,' on the ground
that we lack knowledge both as to the powers
of Nature and as to other spiritual beings
than God. Locke himself defined miracle as
'a sensible operation which, being above the
comprehension of the spectator, and in his
opinion contrary to the established course
of Nature, is taken by him to be divine.'
The subjective aspect of the miraculous is
here emphasised in phrase after phrase; and
its indispensability is indicated in his further
remark that 'it is unavoidable that what is
miracle to one will not be to another.' Thus
Locke, in relation to the main issue, is
at one with Spinoza; but Spinoza, after

trenchantly describing the subjective reference inherent in the notion of the miraculous, proceeded to argue that 'miracle' is only an expression for our ignorance; whereas Locke persisted in the orthodox view that miracle is an essential and a legitimate ground of Christian belief. The causing of belief and the logical grounding of knowledge are, at least on the surface, very different things; but we shall be in a better position to discuss the relation of miracle to either of them when we shall have inquired into the causation of miracle as distinguished from the secondary causation involved in the natural order describable in terms of natural law. To the causal problem I shall devote the main part of my second lecture.

Lecture II

NATURAL AND SUPERNATURAL CAUSATION

In the preceding lecture I considered miracle only in respect of its involving breach of law or uniformity. In so far as a law of Nature is taken to be a *description* of similarities, of sequences and concomitances, it does not explicitly, or on the surface, assert anything about the efficient causation of events, or as to how regularity of succession, etc., is brought about. This is another field of investigation, and one with which we shall be especially concerned to-day. Science, as we have seen, professes nowadays to eliminate causation, in the metaphysical sense, from its sphere of inquiry, though the existence and the possibility of science evidently presuppose a stable causal nexus, a nexus of activities immanent and transeunt in continuant things or substances. A philosophical investigation into the presuppositions of miracle must therefore go further than science, in this restricted sense, can accompany it; for the causation of miracle is one of the most essential elements in the problem raised by alleged occurrence of the miraculous.

The difference between the line of inquiry now to be prosecuted and that to which we have hitherto confined ourselves may be indicated by the observation that irregularity or breach of law as known up to date can perfectly well be conceived as being brought about by Nature's unaided potencies of which at the time we have incomplete knowledge, or, in other words, by secondary causes alone. On the other hand, the relatively settled order of the realm of the natural does not necessarily bespeak absence of supernatural agency or of the continuous volitional activity of God. There is no incompatibility between regularity of Nature and divine activity: Nature's regularity might conceivably be the outcome of continuous divine volition, and Nature's laws be *coutumes de Dieu*. Efficient causation need not be characterised by regularity; regularity need not be the outcome of non-volitional or mechanical behaviour. The antithesis to regularity is irregularity, however caused; the antithesis which we are about to examine, between the supernatural and the natural, the miracle and the settled order, is to be found precisely in respect of mode of causation. And in this connexion regularity and irregularity in turn become

irrelevant; because naturally caused phenomena may be irregular, and supernaturally
caused events may be regular or law-abiding.
It is partly owing to the fact that these two
quite different issues and lines of discussion
were often confused, that the controversy
concerning miracle became the tangle with
which the student of theological thought in
the nineteenth century is familiar. We shall
clarify our obscure problem somewhat if we
endeavour to keep them distinct, and avoid
correlating, as if antithetic, a concept fashioned by analysing the idea of law with one
attained by analysing that of causation.

It will be plain that unless there be some
real antithesis awaiting to be made precise,
in the common sense contrast between the
natural and the supernatural, it is idle to
speak of miracle. To find more precise definition of this vague contrast is our immediate
pursuit. We may enter upon it by eliminating
some obvious sources of superfluous com-
plication.

We are sometimes told that no line of
demarcation between the natural and the
supernatural admits of being drawn. To this
I demur, as it seems to be the outcome of a
mingling of issues which can easily be resolved. It is true that, for the theist, there
is a sense in which all the natural, commonly
so-called, is supernatural. For the theist, the

natural was at first supernaturally caused, *i.e.* divinely created. It is perhaps also divinely maintained or conserved, whatever that may mean. It may certainly, from the theist's point of view, be divinely controlled or providentially ordered; it is expressive of divine and perhaps 'increasing' purpose, and is a means by which such purpose is being fulfilled. I can offer no apology for these expressions 'means' and 'purpose,' though I am aware that some who profess and call themselves theists would only sanction their usage as anthropomorphic euphemisms for nothing at all. To me it seems advisable to cease to speak of God if we are not to mean by the word 'God' a living Spirit with an experience, which of course involves relation to time, and with interest in the time-process or the world's development. To the phrase 'The Absolute' I can attach no meaning unless it be either that of the totality of the existent, or else that of the self-subsistent or underived; and when it is taken in the former sense, as often appears to be the case, and also as equivalent to 'God,' theism seems to me to have been explicitly abandoned.

This digression into personal confession has been necessary in order to indicate precisely the presupposition from which I approach the discussion of the topic before us. To return to that topic, I would submit that however much the natural is steeped in the supernatural, in the ways just now mentioned, there is none the less a sense in which distinction between the natural and the supernatural is called for. Once Nature is created, or created in part, created things must be credited with some relative independence of God, as well as with dependence on His will: for they are 'planted out' existents other than God. We must not speak of *Deus sive Natura*, but of God *and* the world. We must not speak of God as alone 'really' existing, as if there were some other way of existing that is not 'real,' because, whatever 'real' might be taken, in either context, to mean, I fear we should only be talking nonsense in the most literal sense of the word. Theism, I therefore assume, posits both God and a world or a Nature; and *Natura naturata* is not *Natura Naturans*, if the latter phrase denotes God. But at this point I must digress again, because the word 'Nature,' which will henceforth be frequently used, is highly ambiguous. In any profitable discussion concerning Nature, it is therefore essential to distinguish at the outset between its several meanings and to abide by one only. Otherwise we cannot but become victims of the commonest and subtlest kind of fallacy, that of talking of several different things as if they were one, which reduces logic to verbal legerdemain and argumentation to a refined kind of punning.

'Nature' is sometimes used to denote 'all that is,' the whole of actuality, past, present, and even what will be in the future. It must have been used in this sense by Huxley, when he said that if a law of Nature ever becomes confronted with an exception, such as an alleged miracle, we must widen our law so as to include the exception. He plainly implied that we *can* widen the natural law to include the alleged supernatural within the natural: 'we,' of course, being understood to comprise posterity indefinitely future. This pious hope involves abolition of any possible distinction between the supernatural and the natural, and reduces the *miraculum* to the *mirabile*. Such a view may be entertained by the pantheist, the absolutist, or the materialist; and in so far as a man of science cherishes it, it is *quâ* metaphysician of one of these types and not *quâ* scientist. And, we may add, certainly not *quâ* theist. Science proper does not and cannot assert the non-existence of the supernatural; it may be 'atheous,' by the rules of its game, but is not atheistic. Its world or Nature is not proved, or even asserted, to be a 'closed system,' or a dead mechanism and no more; the supposal that it is, is simply science's convention to treat it *as if* it were, and is part of the content of its 'let it be granted.' Science such as knows its own nature and minds its own business, has neither desire nor capacity to establish Huxley's assumption or hope that the natural is absorbent of the supernatural. The theist is, therefore, perfectly free to draw a distinction, if he can, between the two realms; and I shall presently argue that he cannot make use of the word 'Nature' in the sense of 'all that is or will be.'

A second ambiguity in the word 'Nature' arises, in that it is sometimes used to include, sometimes to exclude, man. This, however, will not introduce any disturbing element or turbidity into the present discussion. More important, at least in connexion with the subject of my first lecture and its bearing on theism generally, is a further ambiguity as to which it may be well now to say a word, though the point is but indirectly relevant to our immediate inquiry. It is commonly said that science, in its higher reaches, is a conceptual scheme valid of the perceptual. Laws of Nature, in this case, will be laws about the perceptual world. But it is equally commonly overlooked that what is then designated by the word 'percept' is something very different from the more purely perceptual, and more approximately impressional, objects of concrete individual experience. It is these objects which constitute reality in the one and only sense of 'that blessed word' that begs no question; it is they that are the primary 'reality' from which science constructs its knowledge of an external world. The percepts, so-called, which science accepts as data are, however, the 'things' of common sense, the objects not of individual, but of common or universal, experience; and these are already so far conceptual, and therefore non-perceptual and abstract, as to be common to many and to be what is called 'repeatable.' In the carving of the more ultimately and purely perceptual objects of individual experience into the 'Objects' of common experience, such as The Sun, a profuse shedding of chippings is involved, which science and philosophy, each for its own reason, alike neglect. *Natura non nisi dividendo vincitur.* But is Nature, when thus neatly partitioned into discrete things or petty closed systems; is fact, clipped so as to be amenable to theory, and clipped in accordance with the accidental requirements of the human time-span and of the senses which happen, in man, to be the most highly developed, the same as Nature before science, or even rude common sense, vivisected her? Obviously not. Science's artifact, commonly spoken of as Nature, bears to the Nature actually impressed upon us individually, only the relation of skeleton to body, of diagram to actuality. And the elements of concrete Nature which science selects as essential and calls 'primary qualities,' because they lend themselves to number and lead to the establishing of identities behind diversity, may, for other purposes than that of science, and in respect of Nature's 'meaning'—with which science has no concern—be the least, rather than the most, significant 'utterances' of things. That what science calls Nature is ordered by quantitative law may thus conceivably be, from the point of view of interpretative philosophy, a matter of no profound importance. I must not pursue speculation thus opened out. But it is not without relevance to our whole inquiry to have insisted that when we talk of Nature and laws of Nature, we may inadvertently be confounding quite different things*.

Whatever difference there be between the perceptual phenomena of concrete experience and the conceptual phenomena of science I shall assume as a provisional basis of discussion that, back and behind of both, there is a plurality of things or continuant substances, call them monads or things-*per-se*, or what we like, with determinate natures, activities and relations, the basis of that

* See Note C, p. 100.

relatively settled order, that nexus of secondary causation, that in common parlance is called the natural. This is what I would mean by 'Nature' as a world over and against God. In this Nature there must be immanent and transeunt activity or causation. Science, we have already seen, leaves efficient causation to the metaphysician. Well, we cannot but be metaphysicians; perhaps those who think they are not are the most metaphysical of us all. And certainly, as metaphysicians, we cannot dispense with the categories of substance or continuant and of cause (immanent and transeunt) which Mr Johnson has recently reminded us are not two categories but one, unless we undermine the very presuppositions on which there can be an orderly world to know or we can be in it to know it. Now such a determinate system of existents conceivably might not be a cosmos penetrable by thought, or a world containing any similarities, repetitions, or uniformities. But as a matter of fact it is, and at least for some time has been. And though I have previously argued that any nomic necessity, by which science appears increasingly to replace contingency in the world, has significance not directly of the primary reality presented in individual experience but only of the scientific description thereof, or its skeleton, I would now venture to submit that not only could conceptual science have no validity of the perceptual, or of its noumenal counterpart, but that ultimate reality could not behave *as if* our conceptual laws and theoretical fictions were true, unless in Nature, as I have defined it, there were some cosmic regularity. What now pass for laws of Nature may not necessarily state the whole or the ultimate truth; but they must state some 'function' of it, to appropriate a mathematical term, else such laws could never have been discovered or invented or established. The regularity which scientific laws formulate, however, is not necessarily immutable or permanent. There is epigenesis in the world as well as evolution of the preformationist type: the world is no static block-system but a developing and a plastic thing; and that is partly why tracts of it have not been describable in terms of law. But if Nature herself is thus in part ever *naturans*, she is in part—though not necessarily irrevocably—also *naturata*. There is what Bishop Butler very judiciously called 'a relatively settled order.' And I would call attention to the need to emphasise equally the words 'relatively' and 'settled.' Without the former, we should be back at rationalistic deism: without the latter, we should be back at pre-scientific superstition.

But if Nature is plastic to internal spontaneity: if she can form new habits and possibly to some extent give up old ones (matters as to which science can only be wise after the event), it is a further possibility—and a matter for further contention —that she is also plastic to forces from without. *A priori*, there is room for supplementary creative acts, for miracle, and also for providential guidance of the already created. Such things are possible: but the theological issue to-day, now that the *a priori* issue is a dead one, is whether such things are compossible with the scientific probabilities summed up in the phrase 'reign of law.'

We are now brought in sight of the distinction which I am trying to draw between the natural and the supernatural. On the one hand, there is a Nature which has been planted out, and in which are causal activities other than the creative acts of God by which it was planted out. There are preformed potencies and tendencies intrinsic to Nature. When these are not modified by fresh creative activity, Nature is wholly natural, save in the irrelevant senses previously mentioned. There is a relatively settled, stereotyped, order characterised by routine and regularity. Within this order there may, and there does, emerge the *mirabile*; and as we

saw in the preceding lecture, by reference
to law alone we cannot ever positively say
that a given *mirabile* is also a *miraculum*—
i.e. something not possibly the outcome of
Nature's unaided and preformed potencies.
A miracle, in order to be distinguished in
thought from Nature, from the settled order
which is its necessary background, must
therefore be defined not only as an exception
to law, but as due to supernatural causation.
As I am now using the terms 'natural' and
'supernatural,' *i.e.* as divested of certain
irrelevant associations, natural causation
means the immanent and transeunt action
of created things; supernatural causation
means fresh, direct, unmediated or non-
devolved, intrusive or interpolated, activity
on the part of the Creator. In so far as
Nature is left to her own devices, so to speak,
and behaves *as if* God-forsaken, we are presented with the natural; in so far as new
streams of causation are initiated, or what
would have issued from Nature's potentialities or unaided tendencies is replaced
by something due to divine intervention,
we are confronted with what I am calling
the supernatural. If there be any such new
creative activity, whether production of a
miracle or providential ordering in general,
and if, further, instances of it can be indicated,
then we should be able to define a miracle

without resorting to the subjective qualifi-cation which we saw to be unavoidable so long as we try to conceive of miracle solely in antithesis to law. But so long as we are unable to say what can and what can not be the outcome of Nature's unaided pre-formations and original collocations, then, though we thus get a means of defining what a miracle *would* be, we are brought no nearer to being able to affirm that *miracula*, as distinguished from *mirabilia*, have ever hap-pened. The only practically serviceable definition of a miracle would be, an event *interpreted*, or seeming to call for interpre-tation, in terms of immediate or new divine causation. Then, however, the miracle be-comes the 'sign' only.

Unless the order of created things, especi-ally physical things, were largely left to itself—unless there be *some* truth in the so-called deistic doctrine of an 'Absentee God' —it seems to me impossible to give credence to science or to theism, or to find even a partial and proximate solution of the prob-lem set by the existence of evil in God's world. Yet the distinction between activity devolved upon created things from which the Deity stands a handbreadth off to give free play, and the direct or non-devolved activity of God which I have called the supernatural, has been repudiated; not only by materialists and pantheists, neither of whom can possibly entertain it, but by some theists. For instance, Wendland, the author of a work on miracle that has been widely read and commended, objects to any difference being alleged between mediate and immediate divine activity. He would refer all the activities of Nature to God's direct causation, and so imply that God is the sole cause and that there are no secondary causes. But if this be not explicit pantheism, into which philosophical theism throughout its history has shown a persistent tendency to lapse, it is at least acosmism to the extent of denying a world of continuant things. Conservation of the world becomes re-creation at every instant; there is no *Natura naturata* with autonomy. The apparent nexus between apparent things is mere appearance, and the only real nexus is that between God's volitional fiats: just as in Leibniz's system it was appearance of the immanent evolution of unrelated monads. I will only say of this theory that its disastrous consequences overtake man as well as the world, unless man is to be arbitrarily, and in defiance of all continuity, excluded from Nature; and that it shatters the assumptions or presuppositions on which all scientific induction is actually based.

Theism, I submit, must be sufficiently

tinged with deism to recognise a settled order, and an order in which the causation is not immediate divine creation. And if theology is to continue to be in earnest in ascribing to miracles evidential value as to the supernatural, it must refuse to accept the doctrine that miracles have their *semina occulta*, in the phrase of Augustine, Leibniz, etc., in the natural. The antithesis between the natural and the supernatural which I have indicated, seems essential to theism, and is involved in any concept of miracle such as was wont to be deemed theologically significant. At the same time, theism must zealously retain Butler's qualification of *relatively* settled. This is where it differs from the deism which assumed or implied that God's eternal plan was achieved, and His creative activity exhausted, in creating the world and impressing upon it a system of static or immutable law, so that He became an absentee or mere spectator, and the world a God-forsaken machine.

Assuming now the abstract possibility of miraculous intervention in the natural, and of supernatural guidance thereof, the next step is to ask, in terms of what kind of analogy is such supernatural agency to be conceived or imagined?

It has often been assimilated to what is commonly called human interference with the course of Nature, which is an observable actuality. When, by using a pump, we make water flow upwards, we violate no law of Nature; but, combining forces each of which is purely natural, and which Nature herself does not combine, we produce an effect which Nature herself does not produce. If Nature be construed so as to exclude man, then in such human volitional acts we already see the supernatural. If Nature include man, we are still confronted only with the natural; but in divine activity of similar type we should be presented with the supernatural, for it would serve no purpose to include God in Nature or to call His acts secondary causes. As in the case of analogous human procedure, there need here be no violation or suspension of law, and nothing to put science to confusion, so far as causation is concerned. Supernatural intervention would be a combining, regulating, subordinating, of natural forces, transcending the capacities or intrinsic potentialities of Nature; but the objectionable terms 'interference,' 'violation,' 'suspension,' etc., all of which bespeak the unduly rigorous conception of law that I have stigmatised as pseudo-scientific, become gratuitous. This mode of imaging divine intervention is reasonable, so far as it goes. Doubtless it would need to be supplemented if all alleged miracles were to be causally accounted for. But within limits it affords an alternative to the hypothesis of continual new creation. Beyond those limits, we should need to fall back upon the idea of creative activity. As to that, a theist need have no scruple; inasmuch as he cannot in another connexion dispense with the concept of creation, however unable he may be to elucidate or analogically to explain its con- notation. Indeed the alternatives which we have compared are not mutually exclusive; and whichever we choose to adopt, we alike imply that miracle is not activity from within the nexus of secondary or natural causation, but activity *ab extra* upon it. Such activity *upon* physical Nature, by the way, is all that can be meant by the poetic phrase 'immanence *in*' the physical: at least from the presuppositions of theism as dis- tinguished from pantheism or acosmism.

I have now sketched the ontology of miracle that seems to be presupposed by Christian apologetic of the type that would, in the miraculous, see evidence of super- natural agency. There remains the question whether a miracle, as described in respect of its causation as well as in respect of its relation to law or uniformity, admits of being with certainty recognisable as *miracu- lum* and not merely *mirabile*. I am afraid this question must be answered in the negative. Not indeed because Hume settled the matter. His particular argument for the unknowability of the miraculous will not bear examination, though it seems to have persuaded so acute a thinker as Leslie Stephen. And Kant's is little better when, after the manner of Spinoza, he affirmed dogmatically that God's mode of action is only knowable through the *order* of Nature, and represented that the theistic assertion of miracle annuls the possibility of the theistic idea. He should have said 'the deistic idea'; for he but reproduces the rationalist's pre-judice and inordinate reverence for immu-table law. However, there are more cogent reasons than those adduced by Hume and Kant for the conclusion in question.

So long as the constitution of Nature is not exhaustively known, it is no more pos-sible to assert that a given marvel is beyond the unaided powers of Nature, and that accordingly it evidences with directness and certainty supernatural activity *ab extra*, than to affirm that an event indescribable in terms of natural law, as systematised up to date, is for ever or intrinsically incapable of being subsumed under natural law. The sanguine negative expectation of common sense is by no means the same thing as assurance based on logical grounds; though it is surprising how tenaciously common-sense people persist in treating them as identical. With science's discoveries behind us, and the progress of science into the unknown before us, it behoves us to be chary of setting limits to the extension of our knowledge of the reign of law and of secondary and human causation.

We shall need to revert to the question of the knowability of the miracle when on a future occasion we discuss that of its credibility. I will therefore not now pursue it further. The genus 'supernatural' includes other species than that of the 'miraculous'; for instance, the providential ordering of Nature: and I would now diverge from miracle proper to say a word as to this other kind of divine activity.

The natural world is not to be assumed to be God-forsaken even if miracle, in the more restricted sense, had never happened since its first creation. The sporadic interpolation of new existents, initiating new streams of secondary causation, is not the only kind of divine agency for which theism —or, for that matter, early deism—would find room. That Nature is in part *naturata*, and as such is to some extent left by God to itself, I have already argued to be a presupposition of inductive science and also a condition without which theism itself collapses. But the settled order, to repeat it once more, is to be conceived as relatively settled. The element of deism which theism must retain does not leaven the whole lump; it does not crowd out what has been called divine immanence. Nor, we have next to see, does science deny to theism the right to speak of providential ordering. On the contrary, it has itself suggested lines along which we may imagine some cases of such control to be effected, without involving any stultification of scientific intelligence. Tyndall, to be sure, was unable to give scientific credence to the alteration by the Deity of the direction of the motion of a bit of cloud, because the ramification of the effects might produce consequences of catastrophic dimensions and indefinitely make the course of Nature different from what it otherwise would have been. However momentous this alteration, it may nevertheless be affirmed that, in such a case, science would be none the wiser; as it undoubtedly would have instant cause to be if, *e.g.*, the sun were made to stand still. Other physicists have indicated means by which divine control of matter, at its molecular level, can be scientifically pictured. I will not cite Maxwell's demon, because his activities can be convicted of violating the principle of the conservation of energy. Not that the conservation principle is the sacrosanct thing it used to be: there are eminent physicists who seem to be sitting very loose to it, even in the form in which it is not wont to be mis-stated in text-books. But it will be best to avail oneself of a suggestion that is beyond cavil; and such an one has been furnished by the late Prof. Poynting and others possessed of the highest authority. Events in Nature of the molar order can be supposed to be brought about, which unaided Nature would not bring about, through the alteration of the paths of molecules by force exerted at right angles to their directions. Such forces change neither the mass of the molecule nor the total energy or momentum of the system involved. The deflecting force does no work; yet it produces transformation of energy. And inasmuch as the scientific investigator never watches molecular movements on a cosmic scale, he would, in case of this kind of supernatural intervention, be entirely unable to become aware of any abnormality, of any departure from Nature's relatively settled routine, having taken place; he would discover nothing such as used to be described as suspension or violation of law.

I do not profess to know the limits within which molecular guidance such as Poynting suggested is of use for enabling us to imagine God's control of physical phenomena; but it certainly has relevance to some tracts of the physical, and presumably is applicable to local atmospheric changes. In that case, prayer for fine weather is not to be ruled absurd on specifically *scientific* grounds; if it is to be objected to in the name of religion, it must be for ethical or other reasons. But it is enough to have indicated one way in which supernatural guidance of the physical may be directly effected, suggested by physics itself; it will serve to render more credible to scientific minds the possibility of others. A more important observation, at least in its religious connexion, is that divine action upon the physical may also be mediated through human minds and their volition. Direct *rapport* between the divine and human minds is of course an essential tenet of theism; and if science is not able to assert such *rapport* it is no more able to deny it. Here, however, an indefinite scope is provided for divine modification of Nature's tendency. We know that volition is largely determined by attention, and attention by suggestion; it may also be determined by mental *rapport* of kinds as yet beyond the reach of introspection or of analytical and experimental psychology. We have therefore only to postulate God's operation on the inmost springs of human conduct, and we can understand mediate, in addition to immediate, divine action upon the world;

for human alteration of Nature's course is common fact. There cannot, in the admittedly unfathomed mental life of man, be less than psychology has found: there may very well be much more. But without appealing to the merely possible and unknown, we can easily imagine God's energising in the physical world through the medium of human minds. Conversely, there is no scientific knowledge to forbid the *rapport* between human minds and the divine occasioning His direct action on the physical. There is therefore no *scientific* impediment to the supposition of simple piety that more things may be wrought by prayer than science dreams of. There is no impediment of this kind, indeed, to belief in what are called particular providences and personal messages. But, to be sure, we need here to emphasise the need of 'trying the spirits,' else we open wide the floodgates of 'enthusiasm' and superstition. I am not concerned, however, with any other conditions that may reasonably be thought to be involved in such topics as the answering of prayer concerning physical events and the others to which there has been occasion to allude; all I am contending for is that, so far as natural science is concerned, more possibilities lie open than pseudo-science is wont to recognise. To call attention to the limitations of science and of its bearing on theism is neither to disparage science nor to foster superstition; though it may be to put oneself into a cleft stick.

By way of bringing our discussion, as thus far pursued, to a definite issue, and with a view to preparing the way for consideration, in the remaining lecture, of another aspect of miracle, I will now sum up the conclusions which I have endeavoured to establish and indicate the attitude which they seem to compel us to adopt towards the alleged miraculous.

We have seen that one mark characteristic of all occurrences denoted by the word 'miracle' is that of extraordinariness, which, under pressure from growing science, was refined into that of inexplicability in terms of laws of Nature as formulated at a given time. This mark may be possessed by events without involving any disaccord with scientific knowledge—or, to give the thing its right name—with scientific expectations. It does not, however, serve to distinguish such marvels as traditional theology would call *miracula* from others which it would call only *mirabilia* devoid of theological significance. The only way in which a *miraculum* could theoretically be made distinguishable from a *mirabile* is through proving it to be not causally due to the activity devolved by

God upon created things, or an outcome of Nature's original collocations. Law furnishing no criterion for the differentiation of which we are in search, we have to appeal to mode of causation. It is solely in respect of mode of causation that we can distinguish between the natural event and the supernatural. We have further seen that we can neither define theism, nor solve certain theistic problems, nor account for the existence of inductive science, unless we are in earnest with the contrast between a relatively settled order of delegated causal efficiency and the fresh, direct, energising of God whether displayed in the creation of new entities or in the disposition of those already created and operative. The same contrast must be presupposed, therefore, if there is to be any talk of the miracle. Such supernatural activity cannot be ruled out by science. Thus we have defined miracle ontologically and have vindicated its possibility. But we seem to be as far as ever from being able to know that any given event, however marvellous, is actually a *miraculum* as we have defined it. Further, it is only as we have been led to define it that a miracle can possess evidential value for the establishing of revelation or doctrine; and the consequence of clarifying the pre-scientific notion of miracle, *pari passu* with clarifying those of law, scientific induction,

Nature and reign of law, is that miracle, while possible, becomes unknowable or un-recognisable if it actually occurs. The evi-dential value once ascribed to miracle, and which gave the miracle its theological sig-nificance, has disappeared. In so far as establishing theism is concerned, it has become evident that belief in miracle pre-supposes belief in God.

This, however, is no new discovery; the only novelty that I would claim for our finding is its provedness, its clear certainty. In so far as it was anticipated in earlier generations, it was largely as unproved con-jecture, dogmatic assumption, or, at best, obscurely apprehended and imperfectly de-monstrated truth.

That miracle, in so far as Christian usage of the concept is concerned, presupposes theism, is a part or a corollary of the true conclusion, deduced from false premises by the eighteenth-century deists, that revealed theology presupposes rational or natural theology, though not rational theology such as the deists staked their belief on. The truth of their assertion, however much it became mixed up with error, seems to emerge as soon as misunderstanding of its purport has been put away. The deist was but stating the plain fact that he who cometh to God must first believe that He is, along with the tautology that belief, in order to be rational, must be grounded on reasons, and not merely be produced by causes. Thus, he who would rationally credit an ambassador professing to come from an invisible king, must first satisfy himself that there is such a king: he who would rationally accept the messenger's miraculous works as evidence of his divine mission, must first be in a position to know that such works could not be brought about otherwise than through the direct, or cosmically unmediated, activity of God: he who would trust to the unique spiritual dignity of the messenger as proof of his deity, must have learned beforehand that God is good*. This incontrovertible truth that revealed religion presupposes rational theology, was largely ignored, evaded, or confounded with irrelevant error, throughout the nineteenth century. Only here and there did an apologist explicitly recognise it. Prof. Mozley was one of the few who did; but he nevertheless persisted in the conviction that the miraculous was the essential ground of reasonable Christian faith. Mozley thus represents the re-emergence in the nineteenth century of a change of attitude toward miracle that had taken place long before within orthodox belief as evidenced by Paley's writings.

* I here quote from an article which I contributed to *The Expositor*, Aug. 1924.

Paley had doubtless learned from the deists and Hume that to speak of miracle presupposed belief in God, otherwise grounded. He argues that on the theistic presupposition, miracles are antecedently credible, rather than that they are the ground of theistic belief. But they constituted for him the one solid proof of revealed or Christian religion, and are spoken of as if they were the sole cause of belief in the apostolic age. Thus, in the particular case of its application to miracle, Paley accepts the deistic contention that natural theology is logically prior to revealed; and had not this plain issue been afterwards evaded, Coleridge and the romanticists, Schleiermacher and Ritschl, Mansel and Maurice, not to speak of the innumerable lesser lights who taught the doctrine that religion appeals to the 'whole man' in the sense that it must be judged as to its truth by other faculties than the purely intellectual, could not have written as they did, to whatever truth they may severally have borne witness.

The position then, of orthodox belief concerning miracle, as represented by Mozley, was that revealed religion, or truth historically communicated but not ascertainable by man's unaided reason, could be proved only by miracle, the one evidence of God's activity being involved in alleged revelation. God could indeed impart truth or ideas directly; but the recipient of them, apart from their presentation being accompanied by miracle-working, could have no means of knowing whether they were divinely implanted ideas. If he had evidence enough for his own conviction, he would lack means of persuading others.

If the gist of the argument which I have so far submitted be sound, it will already have been seen that this position has become untenable. We have found that the miracle, in the stringent sense that is required for such evidential functioning as Mozley deemed essential, is something which cannot with certainty be identified as such. Besides the reasons already adduced for this conclusion, we may recall Hume's dictum, turned to so much account by Ritschl, that we cannot attribute greater magnitude to an alleged cause than is just required to produce the given effect. There is therefore no arguing to a divine, as distinguished from a super-human, activity. The evidential value of miracle, as it used to be invoked, even if the phenomenon accounted miraculous be proved by testimony actually to have occurred, must then be denied. Marvellous phenomena may cause faith; they cannot rigorously prove the truth of the message they accompany or that direct divine activity was concerned in their production. The most that can now be claimed for the miracle, in respect of its wonderfulness, is that it is an event which *suggests* divine activity, just as the success of science *suggests* that the postulates underlying induction are true. This brings into emphasis the aspect of miracle expressed in the word 'sign.' A new field of inquiry is thus presented, and one for which place will be found in my concluding lecture.

Lecture III

CREDIBILITY AND ALLEGED
ACTUALITY OF MIRACLE

WE have seen that a miracle, in order to possess the evidential value which theology used to ascribe to it, must be caused by the immediate activity of God. Such activity is compatible with science and its reign of law, and is not antecedently unreasonable from the presuppositions of theism; but that a given event, however marvellous, unquestionably is so caused, can never be asserted so long as our scientific knowledge of Nature is inexhaustive. The wonder, therefore, cannot be used to prove theistic or Christian revelation in the sense of affording rigorous demonstration of doctrine.

Further reasons for this conclusion can be given. The ultimate causation of an event is in all cases something inscrutable to sensory perception, something over and above the mere occurrence or presentation of the event, and something interpretatively read into it rather than inferred from it. A miracle, in fact, is a phenomenon interpreted in terms of a particular hypothesis as to its mode of causation; and its ultimate causation is not matter of observed fact. As to supernatural agency of any kind being involved, we must agree with Baden-Powell when he remarked* that if what is alleged of a miracle is that it is a case of the supernatural, no testimony can reach the supernatural. Testimony can apply only to apparent sensible facts and can only prove an extraordinary occurrence. That the occurrence is due to supernatural causes is entirely dependent on previous belief or assumption. And as to divine, rather than any other superhuman agency being involved, we may add, these antecedent beliefs must be more ample than in the case of supernaturalness in general. Locke objected to the description of miracle current in his time, as 'an extraordinary event performable by God alone,' on the ground that we lack knowledge both as to the powers of Nature and as to spiritual beings other than God. He also demurred, like Baden-Powell at a later day, to the common assertion that the miracle of testimony is 'plainly superhuman' as alleging more than observation can vouch for. Apologists indeed were once greatly concerned to adduce a criterion by which to distinguish between angelic (especially demoniacal) and divine agency; and to do so they required

*Essays and Reviews, p. 107.

to resort to considerations other than physical. This of course implied that our natural
reason is after all the arbiter as to what shall
be called miracle proper. The principle invoked was ethical: beneficial effects argue a
beneficent cause. But even this criterion
fails if Satan can transform himself into an
angel of light.

Thus, as in many other cases, what is
often taken to be bare fact or pure datum,
turns out to be fact shot through with interpretative hypothesis, possibly with fiction;
or datum overlaid with subjective contribu-
tions. And this was sufficiently, if vaguely,
recognised in the distant past. Already in
the time of Paley the apologist had shifted
his ground, and was concerned to show that,
on the presupposition of theism, miracles
were credible. Credence, however, may be
reasonable and even logically rational, or
may be but superstitious credulity. Hence
the whole question of the reasonableness of
Christian belief became involved in the controversy on miracle. We find representatives
of all shades of opinion as to the intellectual
status of belief. Locke, as we shall see,
adhered to the view that miracle was both
object and cause of rational belief; Baden-
Powell, at the other extreme, relegated
miracles to the sphere of faith of the irrational kind, asserting them to be wholly

against reason. We have already found grounds for maintaining that belief in miracle, in respect of its phenomenal occurrence and of its divine causation, is in the abstract as reasonable as the belief of science that the ultimate constituents of Nature are of few kinds and are permanent; and that if the success of science as based on this assumption suggests that the indemonstrable assumption is true, so does theism suggest the antecedent probability of the Creator's energising upon Nature.

But we have entered upon a discussion involving the notion of reason and the reasonable; and in order to thread our way through the maze of bygone controversy it will now be necessary to digress and thresh out a side-issue.

One of the main principles for which the deists of old bravely stood was that reason is the sole instrument for the acquisition and judging of truth, in religion as elsewhere. And this is a statement to which most people of common sense will subscribe, so long as the meaning of 'reason' is left conveniently indefinite. If I may coin a much-wanted word, I would venture the assertion that 'reason' is the most 'multiguous' term in our language; and I would further suggest that a 'law of excluded muddle' (a phrase which I owe to a printer's error) is the greatest desideratum of logic as adapted for the use of writers in the English tongue. 'Reason' means several distinguishable things in Locke, two with the deists, one (or two) in Kant, another in Coleridge. In most other philosophical and theological writers it denotes nothing definite, but now one and now another thing according to the purpose in hand. 'Its signification has varied from common shrewdness to a highly, if arbitrarily, differentiated faculty; from infallible intuition of the self-evident or the axiomatic, to the framing of a working-hypothesis; from divine illumination or divine substance introduced into human nature from without, to a development from within of inherited animal mentality; from logical computation of agreement and difference between ideas, or between the forms of propositions, to discovery of matter of fact for premisses or the weighing of probabilities; from the kind of understanding that is satisfied to regard *Hamlet* as an impression produced by some founts of type, to the interpretation which a man will put upon the world in order to feel at home in it; from the scientific conceiving of identity everywhere we see diversity, to any activity having an end in view or a moral motive behind it. It has meant the fashioning of clear and distinct ideas, the apprehension of universals, the search for unity, the transcending of antinomies or contradictions; and so forth.'* It is little wonder that discussion of the reasonableness of Christian belief, whether as to miracle or as to any other ·issue, has hitherto been attended with some confusion.

But as I have remarked in a previous lecture, we now see that rationality in the strict logical sense, or that reason as operating with the finished product of thought, computing identity, difference, inclusion, etc., amongst ideas and discerning implications between propositions without any regard to their truth about actuality, is one definite meaning of reason, and one sharply differing from the meaning borne by the word when it refers, as it commonly does, to the discovery of true premises, the method of induction, or the interpretation of events. In the latter definite sense or senses, as we have also seen, reason contains at bottom an alogical element, an irrational surd that can never be eliminated, and which enters inevitably into all that we call 'reasonableness.' This result of quite recent analysis had been largely, if vaguely, anticipated. It had been hushed up as if indecent. It now stands for ever nakedly revealed: to convict many who have been most concerned to magnify reason's office of having mis-

* From my article in *The Expositor*, Aug. 1924.

understood reason's nature, and many who have taken its aristocratic origin for granted of having been but ignorant of its plebeian descent and connexions.

It will have been made plain, I hope, in my previous lectures that theology can only appeal to reason in the latter of the two main senses that we have at last been enabled clearly to distinguish. And we shall need to bear this in mind when we talk of theistic or Christian proofs, and as we now proceed to discuss what, for convenience, I have called the subjective aspect of miracle.

We found this aspect—from the first implicit in the primitive mark of impressiveness—inevitably disclosing itself when we tried, for clarity's sake, to isolate the objective significations of miracle. The words 'inexplicable' and 'contrary to law' are tainted with ambiguity. 'Inexplicable' may mean intrinsically irreducible, and therefore irreducible at any time and even for omniscience; or it may mean irreducible to law as known by us up to a certain date. The word was taken in the former sense by the deists who assumed that immutable law could be read off from Nature by him who runs. Science, however, has shut us up to the latter meaning alone, which implies reference to the stage of knowledge attained in a given generation, individually or socially. That 'inexplicable,' when applied to miracle, must bear this meaning was indeed recognised in the age of the deists. Samuel Clarke, *e.g.*, defined a miracle as 'an event which *we* cannot subsume' under law; and I have already quoted Locke's definition in which the personal element is more elaborately emphasised.

We have now to observe that the introduction, into the definition of miracle, of this subjective reference involves dilution of logical proof-value. We are left with but faith-producing as the function of miracle. Rationality has been exchanged for reasonableness; logical certainty for psychological certitude.

The subjective reference of miracle was overlooked not only by the early deists, for whom the core and secret of the universe seemed to be wholly revealed to human reason: it was also overlooked by many controversialists of last century, although in their time it was not only becoming increasingly recognised, but was also receiving exclusive emphasis in some quarters as the basis of a new line of apologetic. Great impetus was given to this latter tendency by the influence of Schleiermacher, who regarded 'miracle' as simply a religious name for an event, even for an evidently natural event if only it possessed the functions of a 'sign.' Similarly as in the case of a wonder, a sign is constituted a sign by individual interpretation. It is unavoidable that what is a sign to one will not be a sign—of God's working—to another. We might say that Schleiermacher, and others after him, rejoiced in the discovery, as he regarded it, that religion in general, and belief in miracle in particular, were primarily matters of individual subjectivity, and that he revelled in irrationalism. Schleiermacher eschewed all attempts, like that of Kant, to make room for reasonable faith. Religious belief was to him a satisfaction of what he called 'feeling,' not of reason. This 'feeling,' which his singularly but sagely unanalytic mind was content to leave without psychological definition, of course contained the cognitional or rational element that he was concerned to dispense with; else he could never have advanced from it to communicable Christian belief and to doctrine even as he conceived it, *i.e.* as sharply distinguished from objective science. Superfluous panic, occasioned by the over-inflated intellectualism of his day, seems to have been the spring of what may be called the 'irrationalism' that was first systematically propounded by Schleiermacher and has persisted in one form after another from his time to our own. S. T. Coleridge, another writer who strongly influenced the thought of the earlier half of the nineteenth century, founded a different, and indeed a much more reasonable, type of irrationalism, by putting upon Kant glosses which would have shocked that philosopher of dry light and meticulous tidiness of system. With reference to the particular department of theology with which we are here concerned, however, Coleridge was conservatively orthodox: 'most readily do I admit,' he writes, 'and most fervently do I contend, that the miracles worked by Christ...both as signs and as wonders,...gave unquestionable proof of his divine character and authority.'

More akin, on this point, to Schleier-macher, was Ritschl. By some of this teacher's adherents, a miracle was described as an event (whether natural or super-natural, it seems, is immaterial) which discloses markedly God's redemptive or pro-vidential activity. This view, again, seems to be the outcome of over-anxiety occasioned by the downfall of rationalistic theology, for which as yet no reasoned substitute was forthcoming such as could be welcomed as a theistic basis for Christianity. In the Ritschlian school, too, as in Schleiermacher, the irrationalist trend is determined by the primary presupposition. Schleiermacher's wholly indefinite 'feeling' is there replaced by the equally indefinite notion of 'value-judgment,' or 'judgment of worth.' What Ritschl meant, or should have meant, by that phrase, has been matter of dispute among his disciples; and the issue of the dispute may be said to be that whatever be the meaning of the phrase it is not what the phrase says. If, as seems to me most probable, value-judgment, as used by Ritschl, is often but an unhappy name for a certain kind of causal judgment, then the Ritschlian estimate of miracle, like that of Schleiermacher, is ultimately determined by unconscious retention in religious faith of the cognitional and existential element which he overtly renounced by resort to the value-concept.

A more recent writer, Wendland, who likewise displays indefiniteness and inconsistency, describes a miracle as an act of God whereby He is known to be living and active. This sounds like a purely objective definition, and in the words 'act of God' and 'known' we seem to be presented dogmatically with notions to which, we have seen, we have no logical right. But we must interpret it in accord with the whole trend of the author's book which, as strongly as Schleiermacher's or the Ritschlian statements, conveys the doctrine that wonders, like events other than wonders, are but signs, or that religious impressiveness is the sole mark of miracle with which theology needs to be concerned.

Once the subjective aspect of the miraculous is thus emphasised to the complete exclusion of the objective, room is found not for reasonable faith only but also for unlimited superstition. Wendland himself is not able to abide by his subjective teaching: for in one passage he finds it necessary to describe miracle as the bringing about of an event which is not implicit in previous states of the world. Certainly, unless that is to be the meaning of miracle, all 'rational' evidential value is cancelled; equally certainly miracle then becomes as unassertible as, in the purely subjective acceptation, the term becomes superfluous.

There is, however, a view intermediate between the two mutually inconsistent opinions from the one to the other of which Wendland vacillates. It found ablest advocacy in the American author, Dr Bushnell, but is perhaps more familiar to English readers through the writings of Westcott, who may have been influenced by Bushnell. These authorities do not repudiate the conception of miracle as a supernaturally caused event, but they put the emphasis on its impressiveness rather than on its abnormality. Unlike Mozley, Westcott would no longer see in miracles the proofs of the divine origin of Christianity, but rather parts of the Christian revelation. They are signs rather than wonders. Their function is to evoke faith, and their import is didactic. Thus, in *The Gospel of Life* (p. 207), Westcott, after admitting that the definitions of miracle which turn upon particular theories as to causation cannot be maintained (*i.e.* so as to be practically serviceable), says: 'The best idea which we can form of a miracle is that of an event or phenomenon which is fitted to suggest to us the action of a personal spiritual power....A miracle, in other words, is what it is characteristically called in the New Testament, a "sign." Its essence lies not so much in what it is in itself as in what it is calculated to indicate.' Thus the miracle becomes part of the content of revelation rather than proof of its divine authority. The only question to which the whole problem is then narrowed is that as to the credibility of gospel testimony in the light of historical and other kinds of modern criticism. That is a question lying beyond the scope of these lectures, which are concerned only with the philosophical presuppositions underlying the various conceptions of the miraculous. But the difficulties raised by critical investigation are more acute to-day than even in Westcott's generation, else he was singularly unalive to their import. Certainly, it is not possible now for the scholar to assume, as Westcott seems to have done, that we have only to recover the pure and original text of New Testament scripture in order to possess, as a basis for Christian dogmatics, a record of indisputable fact free from disputable interpretation. It is precisely the interpretative element of the alleged facts that more recent modernity challenges; and thus the flank of the old conservatism is turned.

But without going into the field of New Testament criticism, we may observe that it is equally necessary, in the case of what may be called the 'sign-theory' of miracle, as in the case of 'wonder-theories,' to raise the general logical issue of knowability and credibility. And as this issue is also involved in older views as to the miraculous, such, *e.g.*, as that defended by Mozley, it will be well to revert to past history and to trace the development of thought concerned with it.

As a representative of the common-sense orthodoxy that survives to-day as an inheritance from the remote past, perhaps none better could be found than Locke. This eminently 'reasonable' yet deeply pious Christian philosopher regarded miracles as credentials given by God to His messenger, so that we, through testimony, are able to know that Christ's revelation is God's. He was fond of quoting 'no man can do these signs...except God be with him.' Miracle, he teaches, is the basis on which Christ's divine mission is always established; and consequently the foundation on which believers in any divine revelation must ultimately bottom their faith. This was later the position of Paley, and again of Mozley: and it represents an attitude still common in minds not wholly unaffected by awareness of New Testament criticism.

If we couple the statements which I have just cited from Locke with his definition of miracle in which the relation to human knowledge and interpretation is so strongly emphasised, we cannot but infer that Locke would class all the evidence for miracles, however overwhelming it seemed to him, with what he called probable knowledge or belief. Now the general problem of the credibility of miracle as probable was raised soon after Locke's day by Hume; and as Hume possessed one of the acutest minds that have investigated the philosophical foundations of theology, it behoves us to consider his utterances. Not that we need seriously to reckon with them, however. For though Hume's essay on miracles is perhaps the work by which he is most widely known, it is the least characteristic of its author. In comparison with his serious and profound *Dialogues concerning Natural Religion*, it is flimsy and even doubtfully sincere. He had himself based all experimental reasoning— all reasoning, that is to say, concerned with matter of fact—on the principle of causality; and the causality-principle on custom or psychological motivation. Yet in the essay on miracles he contends that discrepancy of alleged fact with hitherto uniform experience *ought* never to produce belief in the testimony. 'Ought' surely implies that belief rests on logical grounds: it is only such grounds that can impose a categorical imperative on intellectual acquiescence. Nevertheless, he tells us that no such justification exists for belief as to matter of fact of any kind. Thus, according to his own account of induction and his own theory of causality, Hume is without right to the opinion that no possible evidence can suffice to render belief in the miraculous reasonable. Nor has he any right to speak of a 'fixed order' with which he convicts miracle of being incompatible: on his own showing, anything may conceivably follow upon anything in this world of ours. Hume, indeed, stops short of denying the possibility of miracle; but he labours to prove, what for theology amounts to very much the same thing, that though miracles may occur, we have no right to believe in their occurrence. I have myself been arguing that so long as 'miracle' is taken in its stricter and objective sense, that conclusion is inevitable. But it is not necessarily true if miracle be interpreted only as 'sign,' and belief in its occurrence be admittedly based on probability. However, whether Hume's contention be true or false, his own argument at almost every turn is built on foundations which he was the first to undermine, and some of which he for ever demolished. The principle which he invokes precludes knowledge where knowledge is possible. For his definition of miracle contains the assertion that it must be an event, the like of which had never been observed before, or which is contrary to the entire course of human experience. Experience up to date, one may observe, is equally opposed to the new discovery of science as to the miraculous asserted by religion; it need afford no more than merely negative evidence consequent on instances being previously lacking. Moreover, Hume's whole inquiry is essentially psychological; he drops all reference to superhuman agency which figures in his initial definition of miracle. Save for sound comments on subsidiary points, his argument is of no value. All that it really establishes is that previous uniformity of experience gives no *cause* for belief in the abnormal; it altogether fails to show that uniformity of experience up to date supplies logical grounds for rejecting any testimony for the abnormal, however strong. Whether any such testimony is strong enough to prove alleged abnormalities, is another question*.

For all Hume has said, then, we may still believe that the miracle, regarded as an event irreducible to law *as known*, at the time of its occurrence, and as *suggestive* of immediate divine agency, is theoretically capable of being proved—*i.e.* rendered *probable*, by testimony. And this belief remains reasonable for all that has been said as to the general issue since Hume. Thus, when Mill qualified Hume's conclusion and laid it down that 'whatever is contrary to a complete induction is incredible,' he was equally harmless. For where is there such a thing as a complete induction? The non-uniform is as experienceable as the uniform; and if the question be given the psychological turn which it received in Hume's inquiry, it is as probable that predilection for uniformity may cause belief as unsound as any produced by inordinate enthusiasm for the marvellous. Miracles, in the greatly diluted sense in which

* For some of the foregoing criticisms of Hume I am probably indebted to an article by Dr Broad in *Proceedings of the Aristotelian Society*, 1916–17.

they can now be asserted to be actualities,
must be accepted as facts, for what they are
worth, if sufficient evidence be forthcoming
as to their historical occurrence.

Confining ourselves still to philosophical
presuppositions, we may next consider one
or two implications of the view represented
by Locke which was not made untenable by
Hume's major criticisms. It is sometimes
objected to it that there is no sort of connexion between wonder-working and truth-
revealing. Immediate connexion, certainly,
there is not. Indeed the evangelists foretold
that false Christs would work signs. Such
connexion as Locke maintained must be
mediate. He would doubtless have argued
that miracle-working, in the case of our
Lord, was moral proof, carrying conviction
to common sense, that 'God was with Him.'
The miracles, in other words, proved God's
agency, and God's presence vouched for the
truth of the message which the miracles
accompanied. Perhaps he would have added
that the veracity and beneficence of God
precludes bestowal of miraculous powers on
any but a divinely-sent messenger. It is only
on these lines, so far as I can see, that the
evidential value of miracle, in the problematic sense that Locke asserted it, can be
defended. And I confess that though it may
strongly commend itself to common sense,

the argument seems to me weak. For it involves that at least part of the message, the truth of which was to be based on the signs or wonders, must first be assumed, otherwise there is no criterion by which to rule out merely superhuman or even demoniacal agency. So apart from the difficulties already found to inhere in the assertion that alleged miracle argues the supernatural or divine, a vicious circle is involved. Miracle, in order to be serviceable to Christian apologetics, seems to presuppose much of the Christianity it was invoked to prove.

This question, in turn, leads on to another: that of the antecedent probability of miracle, theism being presupposed. Plainly, in this connexion, we cannot use the word 'probability' in the formal sense in which it denotes a logical relation, or involves reference to a number of instances, or leads to mathematical calculus. It is a psychological, rather than a logical, conception. The probability we are concerned with is similar to that which is involved when the ultimate principles on which induction rests are called probable. The question is, then, whether, theism being granted, we may 'reasonably expect,' as a consequence, the occurrence of miracle in the sense of divine energising, such as would seem to be manifested in Christ's raising the dead by a word, or in His own rising from the grave. If incarnation, however that be interpreted, of God in human nature, be a 'probable' corollary of theism, is the occurrence of miracle in connexion with the incarnation as an event in time, similarly a 'probable' corollary of incarnation? Is it something which we are psychologically constrained— logical necessitation being admittedly out of the question—to regard as either a human need or a divine expediency? That the whole matter is thus psychological, is evidenced by the fact that equally reasonable persons have entertained opposite views with regard to it. Mozley answered the question in the affirmative. The gospel miracles, he said, are connected with the greatest crisis in human history, and so far as we can see they were the necessary accompaniments of, and means to, the accomplishment in time of the eternal purpose of God, that of self-revelation in human nature. And so, perhaps, will judge others whose mentality is predominantly of the type that one may call the historical. On the other hand, those whose presuppositions as to the nature and action of God are coloured rather by reverence for high abstractions, for timelessness or immutability: those who are naturally inclined to disparage the historical as parochial, and the idea of divine ways and means as crudely anthropomorphic, will tend toward the view of the deist or rational theist, and deem the miraculous to be unnecessary or superfluous. It seems to me that there is nothing to choose, from the point of view of logic or rationality, between these two types of mentality. The representative of the one is just as much as the representative of the other the victim of alogical prepossession; and there is no accounting for tastes, nor any logical justification of them. It is usual for the thinker of the one type to call thinkers of the other type 'unspiritual' or 'unphilosophical'—which begs his own position; and it is customary for the other to call the one 'irreligious': which perhaps less obviously begs any question unless the word 'religious' be used in an unhistorical sense such as deprives it of all unique significance. Philosophy is unavoidably a matter of individual predilection, as its whole history reveals, save on the one condition that it sets out from and abides by fact or objective datum, and not from ready-made abstractions in which individual predilection is already involved. But, unfortunately, in the case of the subject with which we have been especially concerned, reference to indubitable fact or to any datum which opponents can accept in common, is an impossibility. I conclude hence that all discussion of the antecedent probability of miracle is futile.

I will therefore not pursue it further, save to illustrate and apply my sweeping conclusion to one or two particular points of dispute. Mozley, I just now said, made much of the expediency of miracle in connexion with the promulgation of Christianity. Lotze, to name one who represents the adverse view, objects to such 'occasionalism,' though he himself could be occasionalist upon occasion. He objects, as it seems to me, on very unconvincing grounds. In its positive aspect, there is something to be said from the point of view of common sense, for Mozley's opinion. But if expediency be asserted of miracle exclusively in so far as it accompanied the inauguration of Christianity, common sense has equal right to demur. If miracles were necessary to beget faith at first, in a credulous generation, they would seem on similar grounds to be equally expedient in these more critical days when scientific and historical knowledge have rendered faith, for many people of good intent, more difficult, and its grounding, for the intellectual conscience, further to seek. Yet miracles 'do not happen'; and if expediency have any voice in the matter, this so far seems to argue that they did not happen.

But it is by no means a peculiarity of

orthodoxy to allow its judgment as to matter of fact to be ruled by arbitrary selectiveness. There is an often-quoted passage about the miraculous in Höffding's *Philosophy of Religion** which illustrates how easily the philosophical critic may, unbeknown to himself, have his mind filled with antecedent assumptions. This writer asserts that, supposing real miracles or deviations from the law-abiding order of Nature to have occurred, 'the concept of God which could be based on this fact would necessarily bear the stamp of imperfection; for a miracle is a makeshift, a way out, something which has to make up for a want in the order of Nature. The ordering of Nature has not been so effected that by it all the divine ends can be attained. God encounters an obstacle within His own order of Nature.' Surely this is the rationalistic prejudice of the old deists over again: the idea of God is that of the immutable and 'perfect' Being, the idea of the world is that of the block universe (a notion, by the way, which Höffding elsewhere rejects), and the idea of law is that of an absolutely settled order which it behoves God to leave well alone. If, on the contrary, the world be characterised by epigenetic evolution; if the world have a derived or devolved activity permitted to it, as relatively independent of

* E.T. pp. 29–30.

its self-limited Creator; and if any of God's creatures are in their lesser way also creators: then, one may ask, why should not God encounter obstacles within His own created world? Is it not inevitable that He will do so? The deists were so shocked at the attribution of anything like arbitrariness to the Deity that, in their zeal to rule it out, they also by implication removed all possibility of God's directivity, of adaptation of immutable purpose to emergent needs. In their haste to eliminate from the idea of God the very anthropic quality of caprice and changefulness, they ascribed to Him the equally anthropic qualities of indifference and impassive obstinacy. Höffding, who in the context from which I have quoted is also concerned to disparage the conception of miracle as anthropomorphic, similarly credits the Deity with the very human trait of law-abidingness; not to speak of indeterminate characteristics such as perfection which do not admit of precise definition at once suitable to his purpose and compatible with the idea of God as a living Spirit. It may be a fact that, as Höffding goes on to say, miracles 'which in former times were a proof and support of religion, are now rather a stumbling-block which its apologists have to defend'; but if miracles are burdens which apologists 'wish themselves well rid of,' it is to be hoped it is not on the grounds which Höffding commends. 'The less we think of the relation between God and the world as a purely external one,' he writes, 'the less there is room for, or possibility of, miracles.' The word 'external' here owes its sting to the spatial metaphor which it involves, but which is precisely the irrelevance to be stripped away if it is to possess philosophical meaning. That meaning is best expressed by such phrases as the *otherness* of the world and God, and the activity of God *upon* the world. These notions, we have seen, are distinctive of theism and are essential to it; consequently Höffding's particular objection to miracle bespeaks the immanence-theology that is indistinguishable from pantheism.

I have invited attention to Höffding's utterances, which are typical of many, because they seem to give expression to the wrong grounds on which Christian theism should disparage the miraculous: grounds of rationalistic theory of knowledge, pantheistic theology, and pseudo-scientific science. If Christian theology would sit loose to miracle, it should do so on grounds consistent with its own theistic presuppositions, not on those of absolutist pantheism. It should ally itself with genuine science, not with the counterfeit that masquerades as science in popularised literature, and at which the well-informed man of science will smile. It should eschew all *a priorism* and renounce all mere predilection, from whatever various causes it may issue. This I take to be the moral of the long controversy about miracle of which I have undertaken a partial study. If in my endeavour to disentangle the philosophical and scientific issues involved, and to show up the false friends which Christian theism has been over-ready at times to trust, I have seemed to some to have drawn my line unduly on the side of conservatism, it is because I am as jealous that Christian apologetics should not identify itself with science falsely so-called, as that it should not flee panic-stricken, now that the old infallibilities have been exploded, to irrationalist enthusiasm, or resort to the blind roads which have of late been mistaken for short cuts to certainty and have become beaten tracks.

In our day, the problem of miracle is narrowed down to the question of evidence for alleged fact—a question largely beyond the pale of the field which I have covered. Yet the conclusions to which I have been led have bearing upon this issue. If they convict the still lingering belief in the impossibility of miracle of being credulous acceptance of philosophically and scientifically groundless dogma, they at the same time indicate that alleged miracle is devoid of all evidential value. Christianity does not presuppose the Christian miracles; they presuppose Christianity, though they are by no means bound up with Christianity. If signs and wonders actually occurred in connexion with its foundation, they are of little significance for theology in our time. Testimony, we have seen, cannot reach to divine agency. And if it once was supposed adequate to establish facts suggestive of causal explanation in terms of such agency, time has effected a great change of opinion. Almost throughout the period of history with which we have necessarily been concerned, the only alternative that could be descried to convincing testimony was that of deliberate fraud. Other alternatives, however, have since emerged. Miraculous interpretation of the natural can arise immediately—witness the angels of Mons—and can no longer be regarded as involving longer lapse of time for afterthought than orthodoxy can concede to adversaries who assert the testimony to be fictitious. Some gospel-miracles are already resolvable into naturally explicable phenomena, and others may yet be resolved. Some are doubtful on grounds of textual and literary criticism; others owe their plausibility to doctrines which are now seen to have their own intrinsic difficulties and questionableness; a few are sometimes deemed shocking for their immorality or their trivial-ness. Such considerations, largely inacces-sible to bygone generations, have reasonably affected the modern attitude of mind toward the miraculous. Secular history and the comparative study of religions have also engendered doubt; but more potent than all these particular causes of distrust is the awakenedness of modern thought to the truth that what used to be accounted an accumulation of bare observed facts is a collection of facts, if facts they be, shot through with hypothetic interpretation which can no longer be accepted on authority as final, or on its own merits as either self-consistent or necessary.

I will conclude then, as I began, by suggesting that the controversy about miracle has become of but historical interest save for its instructiveness as to what are and what are not to be taken for the essential presuppositions and necessary implications of Christian and theistic belief.

NOTE A

DEISM OF THE EIGHTEENTH CENTURY

I HAVE had occasion several times in these lectures to refer to the deists, or at least to those of them such as Toland and Tindal who gave best expression to the philosophical tenets characteristic of deism in its initial stage; and also to indicate one or two prevalent misconceptions as to these writers. I would further say a word as to their place in the history of English theology, which, as it seems to me, has not received due recognition.

Mark Pattison had no difficulty in showing that deism was a thin creed, a cold intellectualism devoid of religious fervour, aloof from missionary enterprise and destitute of practical fruits; but he did not see beneath the surface. Even Leslie Stephen, for all his sympathy with its negations, was not fully alive to the significance of the movement.

I have already spoken of it as the beginning of modernity in English theology, and will further maintain that deism stands to that theology in the relation in which Cartesianism stands to modern philosophy. I do not compare small men with great; it was because deism had the misfortune to be born in minds of mediocre calibre that it was so easily silenced and, as an actual movement, quickly passed into oblivion. But though silenced, it was not answered; and though dead, it yet speaketh. In its championship of freedom of thought as against obedience to authoritative scholasticism, in its adoption of the method of doubt, in its search for certainty instead of groundless opinion (such as, *e.g.*, the Cambridge Platonists had been content with), in its insistence on reason as the sole instrument for acquiring and judging of truth (however inadequate its own conception of reason), deism not only presents close parallels with the system in which we are wont to see the birth of modern philosophy, but also exhibits the first emergence of a method and an outlook such as distinguish modernity from the nearer antiquity. And despite the many obvious short-comings, the obsolete prepossessions, the crude learning, of the deists, they are to be credited with the dis-covery and the clear enunciation of certain principles, fundamental to theology, which abler minds through-out the succeeding century only evaded, confounded, or buried beneath irrelevances. That revealed theology logically presupposes natural (though not of their kind); that reason (though, again, not as they con-ceived it) is the sole arbiter of truth; that the world is a derived existent over-against God endowed with somewhat of delegated activity and autonomy; these are fundamentals of theism which greater but un-clearer minds ignored to such an extent that even to-day, in our universities, philosophy of religion (as the thing is badly described) is treated as a superfluous luxury rather than as the foundation of all theology and the one propaedeutic to dogmatics. Attention to the deists, who seem not to have been read by suc-ceeding generations but to have been forgotten, would have spared the nineteenth century most of its futile movements and systems, and especially the superficial 'immanence' theology of the unguarded and vague kind that cannot differentiate itself from pantheism. Deism is the *fons et origo* of nearly all subsequent and present unrest and discontent; its vague suspicions developed into critical sciences which effected a revolu-tion in theological apologetic. But it is for its few positive tenets, indicated above, that it is of other than historical interest; and it is on account of its having prematurely arrived (largely from false pre-misses, to be sure) at these that I have claimed for deism a position and a significance not wont to be accorded to it.

NOTE B

THE KANTIAN SCIENCE OF NATURE

An universal reign of law, or the supposition that the world is a perfect cosmos, is indeed a precondition or logical presupposition of there being, as Kant thought there actually was, an *a priori* knowledge of Nature characterised by necessity. It is no precondition of the possibility of experience, but only of that kind of experience which Kant called science or knowledge when he affirmed that in every special science of Nature there can be only as much real knowledge as there is mathematics. Our actual science of Nature is now known not to be of the kind that Kant discussed and mistakenly thought to be forthcoming. He was rather concerned with what would be the *a priori* conditions of our thought *if* its product were to be what it actually is not; with how we should be compelled to think if Nature admitted of being rationalised, *i.e.* known so as to admit of categorical prediction and all-penetrating calculation. The intelligibility of Nature, in this sense of being resolvable into homogeneities or identities, as being characterised by simplicity, and as amenable to logical computation, is neither fact datum nor knowledge; it is a *desideratum*. The rationalist wants to be more 'rational' than he can be, and to conceive the world to be more 'rational' than it is; hence he has substituted for the perceptual world of experience, with its element of 'brutality' or alogicality such as is evinced in the irreversibility and the qualitative diversity of the world, a conceptual or ideal world, in which there are identities as distinguished from actual indiscernibles, and various conditions which in actuality cannot be proved to occur. To be 'rational' in this sense, ultimately means to persist in treating the world as if it were what we know it is not. It involves violence to Nature, which it cuts and clips in order to compel it into a semblance of 'rationality.' The so-called 'constitutive' categories of Kant, by which rationalisation of science was to be effected, are now seen to be no less merely 'regulative' than those from which he artificially distinguished them; they are derived from the specific mentality happening to characterise *homo sapiens* —the measure of all things—as an *embodied* being in commerce with a specific environment, and who 'never knows how anthropomorphic he is'; they are not to be assumed essential to reason-*per-se*, so to say, or reason as it is in angels or God.

NOTE C

NATURA NON NISI DIVIDENDO VINCITUR

THE partitioning of what (at the level of individual and concrete experience) appears as a continuum into what (at the level of common experience or science) is a system of separate things, begins in simple perception, where there is already a contribution from 'the mind itself' to 'what is in the senses.' This subjective contribution with which reality or the objective, in the primary sense of those words, is overlaid, and which may be reading in rather than reading off, is vastly increased when, at the social level, we employ explicit categories of the understanding; and the partitioning into percepts, as developed by science, inevitably advances to the microscopic dividing of the macroscopic, in atomic and electron theories. *If* the conceptual objects of science, from the 'thing' to the 'electron,' be abstractive artifacts, ideal distinctions rather than real 'differents,' then natural laws such as that of the inverse square will be on a par with Euclidean laws about triangles, laws *about* fictions, which may or may not have any relation to 'reality,' whether as brute phenomenal fact or noumenal substratum, other than of the 'as if' kind, or than approximate 'applicability.'

The whole question as to the validity of our partitioning, save as a convenience for a specific end and pursuing a desideratum, is really a case of solving one equation between two unknowns. Solution of the problem seems to be a futile quest. The issue does not admit of dogmatic treatment, and all that can be undertaken is to indicate alternative views that have been held with regard to it. Ignorance is none the worse for being learned, or self-conscious, ignorance; therefore it may be profitable to air these opinions.

As to the non-perceptual or conceptual 'fictions' of theoretical physics—such as the electron—it should be observed that though modern sub-atomic physics can present a strong case for its claim to be knowledge as to possible experience or invisible reality, realistic interpretation involves a leap in the dark. An explanation may be sufficient without being the only one possible, and fiction can perfectly well be useful and suggestive and not merely false. That a theory gives (up to date) an adequate representation, does not necessarily imply that it will not be superseded; and it will involve a breach in the continuity of the whole history of physics if, in order to explain anomalies which the future already seems destined to reveal, it be not necessary to credit electrons with lesser electrons 'on their backs to bite 'em,' and so account for their eccentric behaviour. Many physicists of the first order, as well as philosophers who may be considered to have an axe to grind, sit very loose to the realistic creed that electrons, ethers, etc., are actualities behind the phenomenal. And it is to be observed that, supposing their distrust to be well grounded, there is no absolute discontinuity anywhere between the 'fiction' of electronic theory and the 'separate thing' notion of common sense. Moreover, when in physical theory, such as the electro-magnetic theory of Clerk Maxwell, there is established correspondence between its conceptual elements and the perceptual, the correspondence is not necessarily unique: as Prof. Hobson has lately remarked, 'different modes have been suggested of placing into correspondence what can be observed, with the vectors which appear in the equations.'

The fact that we can be said to know is that law and uniformity apply to Nature *as perceived*. It is a further question whether law and uniformity belong to

'Nature' as unrelated to percipients; for we have no direct knowledge of the noumenal or ontal. Some philosophers, *e.g.* Prof. J. Ward, insist that since we know nothing of Nature as out of relation to subjects, to make any predication thereupon is futile. I confess I cannot subscribe to this Kantian agnosticism until proof be forthcoming that the uniformity of experience is wholly due to subjective creation, and is a reading into reality of what is not there. Doubtless *some* uniformity in the world as perceived may be due to our selective attention; it is difficult to believe that the minute uniformities detected by 'disinterested' science are due to subjective interest, unless indeed it is the first step of 'partitioning' that is *fons et origo* of an elaborate falsification. If experience be the result of *rapport* between selves and things-*per-se* (not in the particular sense of Kant), and unless subjective creation (in cognition) be far more extensive than psychology can vouch for, there should be a one-to-one correspondence between the detail of the phenomenon and the detail of the manifested noumenon: so that if regularity characterises phenomena, regularity should characterise noumenal activity. At any rate, then, if there is no warrant for the assumption that uniformity in the world is independent of all experients, there is equally no warrant for the denial that it is. We are on safer ground, however, when we affirm that the uniformity of Nature of which science talks, *i.e.* the uniformity of the Nature which conceptual science has constructed, is a uniformity of a conceptual scheme in which the objects and events are always more or less abstract and ideal. So are we also when, confronted with the notion of a reign of law throughout the universe, we reply that as to the 'totality of things' science knows nothing. It is further true that whereas theoretical science talks of identities, actual experience only knows indiscernibles; and that human experience would encounter much of uniformity even if Nature's ultimate constituents were diverse rather than absolutely alike. There is appearance of uniformity in human affairs where spontaneity and unique individualities are involved: *e.g.* statistical averages have constancy; and Nature's uniformity may be of the same kind, *i.e.* approximate and non-mechanical.

These observations will perhaps illustrate the significance of the assertion that discussion of a reign of law in Nature must necessarily be useless till we have decided what we propose to mean by 'Nature.'

www.ingramcontent.com/pod-product-compliance
Ingram Content Group UK Ltd.
Pitfield, Milton Keynes, MK11 3LW, UK
UKHW042142280225
455719UK00001B/35